U.K.
MONETARY
POLICY

U.K.

MONETARY

POLICY

BY

ERIC B. CHALMERS MA

Visiting lecturer in Monetary Theory
at the City of London College.

GRIFFITH

Printed and Published by
W. P. GRIFFITH & Sons Ltd.
154 CLERKENWELL ROAD,
LONDON E.C.1.
and at
BEDFORD

First Published June 1968

PREFACE

Despite the freely admitted uncertainty among academic economists as to its efficacy, monetary policy has nevertheless been eagerly accepted by governments as an instrument of economic management. Use of the so-called 'monetary weapon' gives a pretence that corrective steps are being taken; and is certainly to be preferred to vote-losing fiscal action. This is a failing common to many countries and it is only at international gatherings that over-reliance on monetary policy by governments is openly condemned.

Part of the price of this over-reliance has been the very high level attained by world interest rates in recent years. This has slowed down housing construction in the industrial nations; while, for the less developed ones, further restricting the availability of capital at a price they can economically afford. Over-reliance on monetary policy has also caused countries, like Britain, to be slow to correct their international payments imbalance, and in so doing have threatened world monetary stability.

This long essay on monetary policy was originally conceived as a series of three articles for one of the banking journals. But when it came to write them, it was found impossible to keep to the stipulated length, without some sacrifice of essential content. The difficulty was increased by a change in editorial policy, involving a reduction in the average length of contributions. After further futile efforts to condense, including those of the assistant editor, I came to the conclusion that, if they would not compress, then the only alternative was to expand the three articles into "a slim volume". Fortunately, at that time there appeared the Prices and Incomes Board Report on "Bank Charges", providing welcome additional material. Later, it was decided to add as an Appendix a re-structured version of a paper delivered by me at a seminar in the Sub-department of International Economics of the University of Surrey. I am grateful to the Lecturer-in-Charge, Mrs. R. R. Troeller, for her helpful comments and criticisms on that occasion.

March 1968
EPSOM   E.B.C.

Contents

PART ONE

TRADITIONAL WEAPONS

Government regulation of the economy by monetary means operates chiefly on the supply of money and credit and the level of interest rates. But as an instrument of government, monetary policy is more politically acceptable than it is economically effective. When the government of the day is reluctantly forced into vote-losing restrictive policies, its inclination is to try monetary weapons first. For part of the charm of these is that the ordinary man in the street does not understand, and is therefore less likely to resent, them—in a way that he certainly *would* resent a 1d on his cigarettes or 6d on income tax.

At such times monetary measures are also represented as providing that 'gentle touch on the brake', which is all that the economy requires. Apart from the fact that for politicians it is the lesser of two evils, monetary policy is also something of a historical relic. It was one of the earliest means of controlling the economy in the days when taxation was low, the public sector small and no government was good government. The fact that it operated through free market forces was also a recommendation.

Not that the shortcomings of monetary policy have gone entirely unnoticed—they were recognised clearly in the Radcliffe Report.[1] And yet since then governments have continued to cling to it, still largely in its unaltered form. It was, of course, argued in November 1964 (and indeed even before then[2]) that there was no time to do anything other than use the tried methods; although there were some of these, success-

ful in the past, which were significantly not tried—
not, that is, until all else had failed.

Since over the past three years the range of fiscal
instruments and direct controls has been considerably
enlarged, there should be an opportunity for reduced
reliance on monetary policy in the future. This is not
to suggest that the monetary aspect can be left out
entirely, for the supply of the means of payment will
always be a crucial factor in the level of demand. In
any case it is not wholly the concept of controlling
the economy by monetary means that has proved
inadequate; it is rather the weapons used which have
been so—and sometimes, it must be added, the way in
which they have been wielded.

[1] Committee on the Working of the Monetary System—Report, Cmnd.
827 HMSO, Conclusion, para 980: monetary measures ' . . . are incapable
by themselves of having an effect sufficiently prompt and far-reaching . . . '

[2] Mr. Harold Wilson speaking at Swansea, January 1964 ' . . . we must
be prepared until our defences can be strengthened in other ways, to use
short term interest rates to staunch any flow of short term capital so as to
safeguard our sterling area reserves'.

1. OBJECTIVES OF MONETARY POLICY

The operation of monetary policy in this country is the responsibility of the Treasury and the Bank of England, known collectively as 'the authorities'[1]. Monetary policy is only one of several ways of regulating the level of demand in the economy: others being fiscal and a wide variety of direct controls, as well as general indicative planning.

The economy can operate at almost any level of national income and employment, depending on the state of aggregate demand. An insufficiency of demand results in unemployment: an excess in inflation. The overall level of demand or purchasing power includes investment, as well as consumption, expenditure. Both of these depend on the volume of money and credit and also its cost.

If the government desires to raise the level of national income up to that of full employment, it does so through monetary means by increasing the money supply and making credit relatively cheap and easy to come by. Conversely, when a state of full employment has been reached it will then be necessary to restrain further increases in money and credit in order to guard against inflation; which, in the absence of any improvement in productivity, will be the likely result of an excess demand situation.

---

[1] The Treasury has however the final say in the matter of monetary policy. In the 1946 Bank of England Nationalisation Act, clause 4 states: 'The Treasury may from time to time give such directions to the Bank as, after consultation with the Governor of the Bank, they think necessary in the public interest'.

External Objectives

Certain aspects of monetary policy also have an external role to play. High interest rates may be necessary at time of worsening balance of payments, and when overseas interest rates are rising, to discourage foreigners from running down their sterling balances or withdrawing short term invested capital, thus adding to the pressures on our reserves. In addition, Bank rate action in this context has long been held to have a significance of its own in reassuring those overseas that the British authorities are determined to deal firmly[1] with an inflationary situation. In recent years however there has been some evidence that this psychological effect of Bank rate has not only been reduced, but perhaps even reversed.

The use of the interest rate weapon for external objectives is not restricted merely to discouraging withdrawal of foreign funds. It may also be used to bring in foreign funds, in order to finance a payments deficit and keep it from causing a drop in reserves. Short term capital from abroad must be swapped into sterling to be employed in this country and to cover the owners of these funds against exchange risk a forward contract will be made at the same time as

---

[1] In his budget speech of March 1952, in which he announced the raising of Bank rate from $2\frac{1}{2}\%$ to 4%, Mr. R. A. Butler claimed that it would 'show to the world that we not only recognise the very serious situation of the country but are determined to deal with it by whatever firm measures may be necessary. . . . ' House of Commons Debate 11/3/52 Cols. 1282–83.

the swap into sterling. The forward deal will be at a less favourable rate, so that there is an element of cost in forward cover which it is usual to express as an annual interest rate in order to better gauge the real return offered by UK short term interest rates.

The gold and foreign currency reserves benefit from the acquisition of foreign funds that have been swapped into sterling, with the forward position of the reserves deteriorating to the same extent. This latter, however, does not become an actual loss until the forward contract matures—and it may in fact be rolled over for a further period if Britain's short term rates continue to be attractive. Furthermore, from the point of view of overseas confidence it is important to remember that it is the current reserve position that is given publicity each month; no details are given of the forward position, which is in any case more complicated and less certain.

2. TECHNIQUES OF CONTROL

Monetary policy made its reappearance in 1951 with the first post-war Conservative administration. The monetary weapons resurrected were those which had been used for many years before the war and which had been glowingly described in the Macmillan Report. (Bank rate, for example, being described as 'a most delicate and beautiful instrument'[1]) Nevertheless, it is rather surprising that weapons of a bygone age should have been applied to the startlingly different world of the mid-twentieth century.

The traditional techniques of monetary policy may be classified into two groups: those attempting to control the supply of money and credit, and those influencing its cost, the rate of interest. Some of these techniques unavoidably affect both the money/credit supply and the rate of interest; but since these two are themselves related this is hardly surprising.

Money and Credit
Cash Ratio
The most important element in money supply today is bank deposits, accounting for roughly £10,000 million out of a total of £12,500 million. The supply of notes and coin provided by the Bank of England and

---

[1] Report of the Committee on Finance and Industry 1931, paragraph 218.

[2] By agreement between the Bank of England and the London clearing banks, the cash ratio was brought down from 10% to 8% on 1st January 1947, when the banks' practice of 'window dressing' was brought to an end by the rule that they had henceforth to maintain the reserve ratio on a *daily* basis.

the Mint is still in a sense relevant, since cash in the banking system must equal 8% of total deposits.[2] It therefore sets a limit of $12\frac{1}{2}$ times to the extent of deposit creation.

Although individual banks cannot create deposits, the banking system as a whole can. Every time £100 is deposited by the public, the bank receiving it need keep only £8 as a reserve against withdrawals. The other £92 will be lent or used to buy investments. Those borrowing will spend the loan by drawing cheques in favour of other people, who in turn will pay these cheques into their own banks. In the same way, those from whom the bank bought investments (usually British government bills or stocks) will have received a cheque in payment, which they will pay into their own banks. Thus, although the original bank still has a deposit liability of £100, it will have lost £92 of this in cash, which will be received as deposits by other banks, who in turn will retain 8%, i.e. just under £7. 10. 0. as a cash reserve and lend or buy investments with the remaining £84. 10. 0. The latter sum will again eventually be received by other banks as deposits, from which they will set aside an 8% reserve and lend out or invest the rest. This process will go on until the point of exhaustion—which, on the basis of an 8% cash reserve, will be $12\frac{1}{2}$ times the original deposit of £100, namely, £1,250. In this example it has been assumed that no cash is lost by the banking system either to the public or to the government; but, to the extent that it is, the cash base for deposit creation is contracted. When cash is lost,

B

the ease with which the banking system can replenish it is, as we shall see later, an important element in interest rate control.

Commercial banks' cash reserves are held partly in their own tills and partly in Bankers' Deposits in the Banking Department of the Bank of England. The banks replenish their tills with new notes and coins by drawing on their balances at the Bank of England. These balances are also used for the settlement of any inter-bank indebtedness remaining after Clearing House operations. Also held in the Bank of England is the government's account, known as Public Deposits. Cash in the banking system may therefore be varied by flows between Bankers' and Public Deposits; such as may result from changes in government taxation in relation to expenditure, or from the government's dealings in its own securities through the Government Broker. This latter method is completely in the realm of monetary policy: the other being more a matter of fiscal policy, which nonetheless has monetary consequences. It is this area of movement between Bankers' and Public Deposits which is of greater significance nowadays in determining the banks' cash position and their potential for credit creation than the physical quantity of notes issued.

It has been fashionable in recent years among monetary theorists to attach more importance to the liquidity ratio, than to the cash ratio. They do so on the grounds that, provided the banks are above their minimum liquidity ratio, any loss of cash can easily be replenished by encashment of liquid assets. But, as will be shown later, the liquidity ratio itself has in practice proved ineffective in curbing excessive credit creation.

Open Market Operations

Sales or purchases of its own securities by a government are known as 'open market operations', being so termed and practised in many countries (in America, for example, there is a 'Federal Open Market Committee'). When the authorities wish to restrain bank lending, they seek to reduce the cash base by being net sellers of gilt-edged securities. It is immaterial whether these are bought by the public or by the banking system itself, since the ultimate effect in both cases is a transfer from Bankers' Deposits to Public Deposits. When the desire is for expansion of bank lending, to raise the level of activity in the economy, then the authorities will inject cash into the private sector by being net purchasers of their own securities. Again it matters little from whom these are bought.

These buying and selling operations are conducted in the market through the Government Broker, departmental holdings being the source of supply or take-up. Many government bodies have funds at their disposal which they invest in government stocks and bills. The National Debt Commissioners so invest the monies coming into the National Insurance Funds, the Post Office and Trustee Savings Banks. The sterling portion of the Exchange Equalisation Account is also invested in government securities, particularly tap Treasury bills; while the Issue Department of the Bank of England holds government stocks as the asset backing for the note issue, in the same way as it formerly held gold.

Liquidity Ratio
Another weapon of monetary control is the liquidity ratio, currently 28%, which also sets a limit on the expansion of bank deposits. Like the cash ratio, the liquidity ratio applies only to the London clearing banks*. Liquid assets include the 8% cash reserve, as well as money at call and short notice, Treasury and commercial bills. Although the banks are never more than a few decimal points above the cash ratio, they may often be as much as 4% above the minimum liquidity ratio, particularly just ahead of the first quarter tax gathering season, when tax payments cause them to lose cash to Public Deposits.

Chief among the banks' liquid assets is the Treasury bill and in addition much of the funds ('call money') lent to the discount market by the commercial banks

---

* These are the eleven banks forming the London Bankers' Clearing House and are the major commercial banks in England and Wales: Barclays, Coutts, District, Glyn Mills, Lloyds, Martins, Midland, National, National Provincial, Westminster and Williams Deacon's. Of these the following have traditionally been regarded as the Big Five: Barclays, Lloyds, Midland, National Provincial and Westminster. But at the time of writing proposed mergers have been announced between a) National Provincial and Westminster and b) Barclays, Lloyds and Martins. (The second merger being the subject of a reference to the Monopolies Commission). If these mergers take place, the Big Five will then obviously become the Big Three.

are invested in such bills. By restricting the available supply of Treasury bills, it was thought that this, like the cash reserve, could set a limit to bank deposits. When this was desired, debt management would include funding operations, replacing bills by sales of stocks. To ensure an adequate supply of liquid assets, when bank deposits were expanding with the economy, unfunding would take place; government borrowing would be more by the issue of bills, than of longer dated government stocks.

Treasury bills are not however the only three months' investment available to banks and discount houses—there is also the commercial bill. The willingness of business to finance itself by such bills (and of the money market to hold them) has in recent years frequently defeated the object of funding operations.

Variation in Reserve Ratios

Variation in the cash and liquidity percentages would obviously alter the multiple by which bank deposits could be created. Although it is quite normal monetary practice in other countries, for example in the USA[1] and Germany to vary reserve ratios; in this country it happens very infrequently and then only downwards, in the direction of relaxation, rather than restraint. Thus, the cash ratio used to be 10%;

---

[1] The Federal Reserve may vary member bank required cash reserve ratios within legal maximum and minimum limits, which currently are:

	Demand Deposits	Time Deposits Savings	Other time
City Banks	10–22%	3–10%	3–10%
Country Banks	6–14%		

but in 1947 it was reduced to 8% and has remained unchanged since that date. As recently as 1963, the minimum liquidity ratio was reduced in two stages from 30% to the present 28%. Although in this country these ratios are traditionally never increased, in the case of the liquidity one a similar effect can be obtained by the device of 'special deposits'.

Special Deposits
Special deposits were announced in July 1958 and first called for towards the end of April 1960, to take effect on 15th June of that year. By this monetary instrument the commercial banks are required to place a certain percentage of their gross deposits with the Banking Department of the Bank of England, where they earn interest at the prevailing Treasury bill rate. Such calls are usually in terms of 1% of gross deposits ($\frac{1}{2}$% for the Scottish banks) and may be followed by further calls; the maximum so far reached being 3% in 1961. Resort was made to special deposits again in April 1965, with a second call coming in July 1966.

These special deposits are expressly not to be included by the banks when calculating their liquidity position and therefore in effect increase the minimum liquidity ratio. Thus, they not only deny that part of deposits from employment as advances, but also reduce the maximum extent to which bank deposits may grow. Special deposits is also a useful device to make control over the supply of cash to the banking system bear more directly on bank lending, since the liquidity ratio can be brought nearer to minimum and thus prevent any cash loss being too readily made good by turning liquid assets into money. With this no longer possible, the banks must sell investments; or, better still, from the authorities' point of view, recall advances.

Requests and Instructions

The most direct way of controlling the supply of money and credit has also proved to be the most effective. The Act nationalising the Bank of England gave it power to issue instructions to the banks as to how they should in general conduct their business, although not as regards their relationship with individual customers.[1]

Requests from the Governor to the banking system are most frequently made with reference to bank advances. The banks may be asked to give priority in the granting of advances to certain business activities, such as exporting; and to withhold advances from categories less desirable in the national interest, such

---

[1] Bank of England Act 1946 Sect. 4 (3):

The Bank, if they think it necessary in the public interest, may request information from and make recommendations to bankers, and may, if so authorised by the Treasury, issue directions to any banker for the purpose of securing that effect is given to any such request or recommendation: Provided that:—

(a) no such request or recommendations shall be made with respect to the affairs of any particular customer of a banker; and

(b) before authorising the issue of any such directions the Treasury shall give the banker concerned, or such person as appears to them to represent him, an opportunity of making representations with respect thereto.

21

as importing and loans for consumption. The most severe form the request can take, from the banks' point of view, is that imposing a quantitative limit on their lending over a certain period of time.

Requests have not however always related to advances; for example, the banks have been asked not to sell, or even to take up, government securities, when the authorities either wanted support for the gilt-edged market, or during some massive funding operation, as in 1951.

Hire Purchase Regulations.

Another instrument for controlling the volume of credit is variation in the terms of hire purchase agreements. Such changes are often announced by the Chancellor of the Exchequer as part of a package of measures. When a reduction in credit is desired, hire purchase initial deposits are increased and repayment periods shortened; with the reverse happening when there is a desire to stimulate consumer spending on durables.

Interest Rates

The monetary techniques described so far have all been concerned with the expansion or contraction of money and credit. The authorities may also seek to influence the demand for credit by operating upon its price, the rate of interest. In this context some of the monetary instruments already described will reappear again briefly.

The principal instrument whereby the authorities may bring about a change in interest rates is through Bank rate, the use of which influences many other short term rates—not only that on Treasury bills, but also commercial bills and the rates offered by local authorities and finance houses for three months' deposits. Movements in these short term rates ultimately get reflected in those of the medium and long term, although not always to the full extent.

Bank Rate

Bank rate is the rate of interest charged by the Bank of England when it lends from its Discount Office ('at the front door') to the discount market, either on the security of bills and short-dated government securities or when it re-discounts bills. In doing so, the Bank of England acts as a 'lender of last resort' and provides the necessary backing for confidence in the whole system of banking and credit. Borrowing from the Discount Office is however on penal terms i.e. above prevailing market rates and normally for seven days[1]. When assistance is made available only on this basis, the authorities obviously want to see some rise in UK short term interest rates.

The discount market consists of some twelve financial companies who make their living by borrowing on a day-to-day basis from the banks (and others)

---

[1] Towards the end of June 1966 the practice was introduced of lending at Bank Rate for one day. In September of the same year the Bank of England, in addition, began lending below Bank Rate, although still above market rates. In August 1967 seven day lending, which had always before been at Bank Rate, or above, was carried out at a rate below Bank Rate.

and employing the funds so borrowed in holding Treasury (usually 3 months) and commercial bills, as well as government stocks (of less than five years to maturity). Normally, the discount market obtains its funds at an interest rate cost[1] below what it earns on the assets it holds, this being particularly so during a period of falling interest rates.

---

[1]The lowest rate charged the discount houses by the banks is the 'call money rate', which is $\frac{3}{8}\%$ above what the banks themselves pay on deposit account i.e., Bank rate, less 2%.

TABLE 1

Post-war Movements in Bank Rate

		%			%
1951	Nov. 8	$2\frac{1}{2}$	1961	July 26	7
1952	Mar. 12	4		Oct. 5	$6\frac{1}{2}$
1953	Sept. 17	$3\frac{1}{2}$		Nov. 2	6
1954	May 13	3	1962	Mar. 8	$5\frac{1}{2}$
1955	Jan. 27	$3\frac{1}{2}$		Mar. 22	5
	Feb. 24	$4\frac{1}{2}$		April 26	$4\frac{1}{2}$
1956	Feb. 16	$5\frac{1}{2}$	1963	Jan. 3	4
1957	Feb. 7	5	1964	Feb. 27	5
	Sept. 19	7		Nov. 23	7
1958	Mar. 20	6	1965	June 3	6
	May 22	$5\frac{1}{2}$	1966	July 14	7
	June 19	5	1967	Jan. 26	$6\frac{1}{2}$
	Aug. 14	$4\frac{1}{2}$		Mar. 16	6
	Nov. 20	4		May 4	$5\frac{1}{2}$
1960	Jan. 21	5		Oct. 19	6
	June 23	6		Nov. 20	8
	Oct. 27	$5\frac{1}{2}$	1968	Mar. 21	$7\frac{1}{2}$
	Dec. 8	5			

Treasury Bill Rate

When lack of sufficient funds from the banking system (because the banks themselves are short of cash) forces the discount market to use its unique privilege of borrowing from the Bank of England, the price which may be demanded for such borrowing, namely Bank rate, will be above the rate currently being earned on many of the discount houses' assets, particularly bills. The subsequent reaction of the discount market, after it has borrowed from 'the lender of last resort', is to lower its bid at the next Treasury bill tender (every Friday), thereby increasing the rate of interest on Treasury bills; and this in turn will react on rates earned on other bills. The more frequently the discount market is forced to borrow at Bank rate, the more likely is the Treasury bill rate to rise.

On average the Treasury bill rate keeps around a $\frac{1}{2}\%$ below Bank rate. But when reduction in Bank rate is expected, the gap between the two will be greater than this, sometimes as much as $\frac{3}{4}\%$. At other times, when the authorities are anxious to keep short term rates as high as possible, or when Bank rate is expected to be increased, the Treasury bill rate may be only a $\frac{1}{4}\%$ below Bank rate. Towards the end of September 1967 the Treasury bill rate rose to within $1/32\%$ of Bank rate, as the Bank of England Bulletin remarked ' . . . the smallest margin for a great many years.'

Special Device

There is even a special device, little used however, to

ensure close proximity between Bank rate and the yield on Treasury bills. The discount market can be charged as much as $\frac{1}{2}\%$ to 1% above Bank rate for assistance given 'at the front door' and by this technique the Treasury bill rate can be brought very close to Bank rate indeed, without affecting those other short term rates which are conventionally linked to Bank rate. But this, of course, enhances the attraction of the Treasury bill by comparison with other short term investments (particularly those formally tied to Bank rate); so that the number of outside bidders at the tender may increase, forcing the discount market to raise its bid and so bring down the bill rate again. Thus the device can be self-defeating.

Bank Rate Increase
If the authorities wish for still higher bill rates, Bank rate itself must be increased. (The prevailing Bank rate being announced every Thursday, around 11.45 a.m.) Such an increase also brings up those rates formerly linked to Bank rate, such as that charged by the commercial banks for advances (minimum of Bank rate plus 1%; except nationalised industries who are charged Bank rate) and the rate the banks pay on deposit accounts (Bank rate less 2%). There are other rates, like those of the building societies, which also tend to keep in line with Bank rate, although not quite so immediately.

Making Bank Rate Effective
For the Bank rate weapon to operate, the discount market must of course come to the Bank for assistance.

There are ways by which the authorities themselves can see that this happens (thus 'making Bank rate effective'). They can take action, including open market sales, which causes a rundown of Bankers' Deposits in the Banking Department of the Bank of England. This may bring the banks' cash below the 8% minimum, leading them to reduce either their lending at call to the discount market, or the amount of bills they can take from the market. If the discount market cannot obtain funds elsewhere, then it must turn to the 'lender of last resort'.

Back Door Assistance

When cash stringency arises, but there is no wish on the part of the authorities for a rise in interest rates, they will be willing to give assistance at prevailing market rates; that is, charging the money market the same rate as it is earning on Treasury bills ·of recent issue. This is termed lending at the 'back door' of the Bank of England, being channelled through the 'special buyer' (the smallest of the discount houses, Seccombe, Marshall & Campion Ltd.) who acts as a sort of government broker, buying bills, either from the discount market ('direct') or from the commercial banks themselves ('indirect'), if the bills of the maturity which the authorities wish to buy are held by them. When the money market has a cash surplus, the 'special buyer' may become a seller of bills from departmental portfolios. In this way there is a certain flow between the 'tender' and the 'tap' categories of Treasury bills ('tap' bills being those going direct to government departments and not being issued through the weekly tender).

Other Official Influences on Interest Rates

In addition to varying the banks' cash position, open market operations may also, depending on the state of demand in the stock market, have an effect on interest rates (particularly those of the long term), as also will debt management operations in general. The authorities may endeavour to give a lead to the market by the coupon rate and yield on new issues of government stock and by fixing of the 'tap' price on existing issues. The Bank of England's control over the timing (and, in the case of some borrowers, the terms) of other new issues is again a factor on the supply side affecting interest rates. Some rates are not left to be determined by the market but are directly fixed by the government. Among such are the rates offered on investments for small savers, such as Development Bonds and Savings Certificates, as well as Tax Reserve Certificates. In addition, the government of course fixes the rates charged for loans to local authorities from the Public Works Loan Board. At times the authorities have also sought to exert some influence on the rates offered by building societies to depositors.

3. External Monetary Policy

The description given so far has largely been concerned with the weapons of domestic monetary policy; those designed to regulate the internal economy. Nevertheless, as we have already seen, these often have external repercussions and indeed in recent years some of them have increasingly been directed to this end. Notable in this category is interest rate policy which is expressly designed to finance balance of payments deficits by short term borrowing from non-residents.

But, in addition, there are other policies, which, although they quite properly come within the designation "monetary", are nevertheless more concerned with Britain's external account and in many cases are quite specific to the narrower field of "foreign exchange". These have little to do with the regulation of the domestic economy and for this reason they will be dealt with only very briefly.

To fulfil Britain's IMF membership obligation, the Bank of England intervenes in the foreign exchange market to keep the spot rate against the dollar within 1% on either side of the par value of $2.40 = £1. For a considerable part of the 'sixties the Bank also intervened in the forward exchange market (although in this there is no IMF obligation). It did so by supporting the forward sterling rate to keep down the cost of cover on foreign funds invested short term in this country. While normally the cost of such forward intervention is quite low, it naturally assumes gigantic proportions if a downward adjustment in the exchange rate does come about, for example, by devaluation. Since the November 1967 devaluation of sterling the Bank of England has in fact abandoned its practice of intervention in the forward market.

Although certainly a very major recent event, the subject of devaluation is outwith the scope of this present study. Once again, it is primarily a matter of external monetary policy, although obviously having implications for the internal rate of inflation. Furthermore, devaluation cannot be regarded as part of *continuous* UK monetary policy: it is (it is to be hoped) more of a once-and-for-all major upheaval.

Another form of intervention, which the Bank of England has engaged in during the 'sixties, has been as agent for the Gold Pool (only recently disbanded following the mid-March 1968 gold/dollar crisis). This intervention, which has now obviously been abandoned, was designed to keep the price of gold in the London gold market from rising too far above the official US price of $35 to the fine ounce, and in doing so causing buyers to increasingly satisfy their requirements by drawing upon the US gold stock. This aspect of Bank of England monetary policy was therefore primarily concerned with preserving the external value of the US dollar, although the fortunes of sterling were naturally closely linked with this.

Another area of external monetary policy, which has been in existence for very much longer, is of course the Sterling Area, set up after Britain left the Gold

c

Standard in 1931. Sterling Area members agree to accept sterling freely in settlement of transactions between one another. They should also pass on any gold and foreign currency earnings, arising from their trade with the non-sterling world, to the central reserves held in the Exchange Equalisation Account in London and managed by the Bank of England. In return they receive a sterling balance, and thus substantially hold their reserves in sterling. The existence of the Sterling Area therefore makes a very important contribution to bolstering the external value of sterling. Of course, Overseas Sterling Area owned sterling balances, together with those of the Non-Sterling Area, do constitute a potential claim on Britain's very much smaller gold reserve. However, this dangerous situation does not really arise from the existence of the Sterling Area as such, but from the extent to which in recent years Overseas Sterling Area countries have financed Britain's balance of payments deficits.

Also in the field of external monetary policy there is, lastly, the system of exchange control administered by the Bank of England on behalf of the Treasury. Foreign exchange controls are largely designed to arrest deterioration in Britain's international payments and therefore to protect her reserves. Many of the foreign exchange controls introduced or reimposed in the 'sixties have been designed to diminish outflow of long term capital, on direct and portfolio account, both to the Sterling Area and to the non-Sterling world. In some cases the regulations have attempted to encourage long term capital inflow into Britain. Expenditure on travel outside the Sterling Area has also been limited since July 1966.

PART TWO

EFFECTIVENESS OF MONETARY POLICY

1. USE OF MONETARY WEAPONS 1963-65

Having described the traditional monetary weapons, in this second part we examine their effectiveness, before going on to consider the need for change. In trying to deal with the adverse balance of payments, which developed from the middle of 1963, most of the traditional monetary weapons were employed.

Even before the deficit in our payments appeared, the device to charge the discount market $\frac{1}{2}\%$ to 1% above Bank rate was resurrected at the beginning of 1963, in order that UK short term rates could be kept high for external purposes, without necessarily raising Bank rate and the cost of credit internally. This device was employed only once, on the 19th March 1963. Bank rate at that time was at the low level of 4% and the use of the device brought the Treasury bill rate up to within $\frac{1}{4}\%$ of Bank rate, the bill rate having been $3\frac{1}{2}\%$ at the beginning of the year.

On the 27th February 1964 Bank rate itself was increased from 4% to 5%; and then later, on the 23rd November, it was moved up to the crisis level of 7%. The first of these upward movements in Bank rate took the Treasury bill rate up to $4\cdot35\%$ but during the third quarter of 1964, just before the increase in Bank rate to 7%, it was once again within $\frac{1}{4}\%$ of Bank rate; without any further use of the special device. Frequently, during 1964 and 1965, the discount market was forced to borrow from the Bank of England at Bank rate and it was this which kept the Treasury bill rate up so near to it.

In addition to interest rates, many of the other monetary weapons were also employed. To restrict the liquid assets base for growth of bank deposits, the supply of Treasury bills was curtailed from October 1964 onwards. An official credit squeeze was not introduced until the 8th of December, when the Governor of the Bank of England wrote to the clearing banks asking them to restrict the amount of their loans given for property development, hire purchase and personal use. Top priority in extending loans was to be given to assist the financing of exports and investment by manufacturing industry. This desire on the part of the authorities for selectivity in bank lending was underlined by a call for 1% special deposits on the 29th April 1965.

Shortly after this, in May there followed a second letter to the clearing banks, imposing a quantitative limit on the extent to which bank advances could grow further: loans to the private sector were not to rise over the coming twelve months by more than 5% over the level reached at March 1965.[1] The banks were also asked to limit the amount of their commercial bill holdings. A week later, similar appeals for restraint, particularly with regard to the creation and holding of commercial bills, were addressed to the discount market and the merchant banks. To enforce this, the central bank reduced the proportion of inland commercial bills it was prepared to take from the discount market as security when financial help was being given.

---

[1] Subsequently this was extended beyond March 1966 and the restriction was not lifted until the April 1967 Budget.

2. EFFECTIVENESS ASSESSED

But although there was this fairly extensive use of monetary weapons, it was in the main ineffective, the proof of this being the continuation of the deficit and the eventual need to resort to more drastic measures.

Externally

Initially, interest rate policy did protect our reserves from the consequences of the payments deficit (see Table 2). In the first half of 1964, the authorities' policy of high short term rates, brought about by forcing the discount market into the Bank and by increasing Bank rate itself, enabled our balance of payments deficit during that period to be largely financed by a build-up of sterling balances and an inflow of short term capital. The deficit was not at all reflected in our gold and currency reserves; in fact they rose by £17 million. Thus, for external purposes, in the early part of the crisis, traditional monetary methods had on the face of it been successful.

However, in the second half of the year, overseas' opinion grew concerned about the continuance, and indeed further growth, of the deficit. The panic raising on Monday 23rd November 1964 of Bank rate to the emergency level of 7% did nothing to shore up confidence in sterling, but merely confirmed foreign suspicions, particularly since the increase had not been made on the customary Thursday. Even with a 7% Bank rate in force, the pressure on sterling continued: "On the 24th and 25th November, spot sales of sterling recommenced on a still larger scale . . . "[1]

[1]Bank of England Quarterly Bulletin, December 1964, page 256.

TABLE 2

FINANCING OF BALANCE OF PAYMENTS DEFICIT DURING 1st HALF 1964

£s million

1964	Balance of Payments on Current and Long Term Capital A/C	Sterling Balances	Short-term Capital Movements	Reserves of Gold and Convertible Currencies
1st Quarter	− 148	+ 66	+ 32	+ 1
2nd Quarter	− 166	+ 103	+ 77	+ 16

Source: Economic Trends. HMSO.

Note: In the first half of 1964 the balancing item was favourable to the extent of £54 million. Although this item is officially defined as merely representing the net total of the errors and omissions in all other items, a large part of this is in fact unrecorded capital movements, so that the short term capital inflow in the first half of 1964 was somewhat larger than the £109 m. identified above.

Later on, the power of UK short term interest rate policy to prevent withdrawal of foreign funds was considerably diminished by the upward movement in overseas interest rates, which had begun to take place from the second half of 1965 and continued throughout practically the whole of 1966, reaching a peak around November. But before this, towards the end of 1964 and during the first half of 1965, there had been a considerable differential between the euro-dollar[1] rate and three months' deposits with UK local authorities and H.P. finance houses. At this time the euro-dollar rate was around $4\frac{1}{2}\%$, but by the end of 1966 it had moved up to $7\frac{1}{8}\%$ and was then very little below comparable UK short term rates, and not enough to compensate for the cost of forward cover. It would seem therefore that the UK authorities' traditional Bank rate action eventually triggered off a rise in world interest rates, which gained impetus from other factors.[2] When this happened the interest rate weapon ceased to be effective in the external sphere.

Internally

Traditional monetary weapons were even less effective internally. The supply of money and credit grew at a faster rate than real gross national product (see Table 3), with the result that during the years 1963 to 1965 the annual average rate of inflation was nearly 4%.

[1] See Appendix, page 100 for 'Monetary Policy Aspects of the Euro-Dollar'.

[2] Among these were the inflationary pressures in America created by the Vietnam War and the increased demand on world capital markets due to the coincidence of upturns in fixed capital formation in the UK, USA and Western Germany.

TABLE 3

GROWTH IN MONEY AND CREDIT

	Transactions		Note Supply		Bank Cash				Credit		Inflation	
	Real Gross National Product £m.	% increase	Note Supply £m.	% increase	Till Money and Balances at Bank of England £m.	% increase	Bank Advances[1] £m.	% increase	Hire Purchase Debt Outstanding[2] £m.	% increase	Retail Prices Index £m.	% increase
1962	22,818		2,327		623		3,408		569		101·6	
1963	23,735	+4	2,398	+3	647	+4	3,880	+14	614	+8	103·6	+2
1964	25,100	+6	2,562	+7	696	+7½	4,328	+12	754	+23	107·0	+3½
1965	25,749	+2½	2,727	+6	739	+6	4,653	+7	836	+11	112·1	+5
65/62		+13		+17		+19		+37		+47		+11

[1] London clearing banks, monthly averages.
[2] Owed directly to finance houses.

Sources: Monthly Digest, Financial Statistics, HMSO.

Between 1962 and 1965 real Gross National Product rose by 13%, but bank advances increased by 37% and hire purchase debt outstanding rose as much as 47%. Retail prices went up during this period by 11%.

This inflation was not, at least before 1965, due to any over-expansion by the authorities of the note issue. During 1963 and 1964 the increase in notes in circulation was no greater than the growth in GNP. It was only in 1965 that note creation was excessive in relation to GNP growth, largely because the note issue continued to increase at the same rate as the previous year, while GNP growth rate fell by more than half.

Nor could the inflation be much attributed to a too rapid rise in government expenditure, in relation to revenue, resulting in an excessive enlargement of the banking system's cash base. Despite the rundown in bank holdings of government stocks, till money and Bankers' balances increased by only 19 per cent during the period. While this was admittedly half as fast again as the real growth in GNP, it was less than that in terms of current prices and much less than the growth of credit.

We are therefore left with the conclusion that the inflationary expansion in the money and credit supply in relation to real GNP was largely due to excessive bank advances and hire purchase lending, which monetary policy had been too slow in bringing under control.

3. REASONS FOR FAILURE

There were several general factors contributing to the ineffectiveness of monetary policy in arresting the deterioration in our balance of payments and curbing inflation at home. First of all, the problem to be dealt with, in terms of the size of the payments deficit, was much greater. This partly reflected a second general cause, namely that corrective measures were longer in coming, due perhaps to a feeling in some quarters that the action in July 1961 had been too precipitate. And for a long time monetary measures were the only restrictive action taken by the authorities. This was to ignore the warning given in the Radcliffe Report, where it was emphasised that monetary measures 'are not so much a policy in themselves as a part of one general economic policy which includes among its instruments fiscal and monetary measures and direct physical controls.'[1] Earlier, the Report had stressed that, since the authorities had usually favoured a 'package' approach in restrictive measures, there was no evidence that any particular technique by itself would be sufficient.[2]

Incredibly, some of the monetary weapons were even used in a manner opposed to the main drift of official policy. Although in the second half of 1963 we had already moved into balance of payments deficit, the liquidity ratio was reduced to 28% in October 1963; this was certainly not the time to give scope for further expansion of bank deposits. Open market operations throughout most of 1964 were in the wrong direction;

[1] Radcliffe Report, para. 980.
[2] ibid, para. 434.

44

the authorities being largely net purchasers of stock, thus injecting more cash into the private sector, when they should have been net sellers to contract the cash base of the banking system.

Evasion by Financial Institutions
Monetary policy also failed because its impact was often evaded by financial institutions. The attempt by the authorities through reducing the volume of Treasury bills to restrict the liquid assets base, and thus hold the growth of bank deposits in check, was avoided by the substitution of commercial bills in the liquid assets category (see Table 4). When the authorities requested a curtailment of lending by way of advances, the merchant banks instead provided credit by way of bills of exchange. The commercial banks' response to official pressure to restrict advances was to sell securities, rather than call back their loans: for example, from the first request from the Bank of England in December 1964 until May of 1965 the clearing banks ran down their investments by £130 million, increasing their advances by around the same amount (see Table 4).

Merchant and foreign banks in London were able to increase the supply of credit in Britain by obtaining deposits from foreigners. This was mainly done by borrowing euro-dollars* and switching them into sterling for on-lending to finance houses and local authorities. This switching reached its greatest extent

*See Appendix, page 100 for 'Monetary Policy Aspects of the Euro-Dollar'.

TABLE 4

LONDON CLEARING BANKS

				Treasury Bills	UK Commercial Bills
				£s million	
1964 April 15th	..	..	..	731	291
1965 April 21st	..	..	..	457	418

			Investment in Brit. Govt. Securities	Gross Advances
			£s million	
1964 December 16th	..	..	1,056	4,760
1965 January 20th	..	..	1,021	4,639
February 17th	..	..	966	4,749
March 17th ..	..	..	924	4,854
April 21st	..	..	899	4,976
May 19th	..	..	923	4,871

Source: Financial Statistics HMSO.

(at least £400 million) during the first quarter of 1965, exactly the time when the authorities became very concerned about the excessive growth of credit within the British economy. Although the clearing banks themselves do not switch euro-dollars into sterling, the national income generation effect resulting from such activity by the other banking institutions undoubtedly also creates deposits for the clearing banks.

The hire purchase finance companies exceeded the 5% official limit imposed on the growth of their lending during the financial year 1965/66. The June 1966 Bank of England Quarterly Bulletin remarked upon this: ' . . . the finance houses, as a group, did not succeed in meeting the Governor's request that their financing of the private sector should not rise by more than about 5% in the year ending in March 1966: total lending . . . grew by . . . $7\frac{1}{2}$%, over the year.'

D

4. RECENT CHANGES

Eventually in the spring of 1965, many of these loop-holes were closed by the authorities. The Governor's requests were addressed to all the major financial institutions, not just the clearing banks. The restriction on lending was applied to commercial bills as well as bank advances. The Bank of England reduced the proportion of commercial bills it was prepared to take in the package of bills deposited by the discount houses as security when seeking assistance. Then, in order to give the authorities' power to influence the Treasury bill rate greater sensitivity, lending to the discount market at 'the front door' began to be given below Bank rate and for a shorter period than seven days.

Flexible Use of Special Deposits
In his April 1967 Budget speech the Chancellor lifted the 105% ceiling, which had been imposed on bank advances in May 1965. Deflation had already brought advances well below the ceiling; so that, in the words of Mr. Callaghan: 'to continue it . . . would not be effective'. He went on to say that an alternative means of restraint on banking lending existed in the system of 'special deposits' which he said would be 'used in future in a new and more flexible manner, so that a call for Special Deposits should no longer be regarded as a crisis measure, but as a routine adjustment to conditions as they develop. The object will be to maintain a continuous control over bank lending.' As we have already seen, this latter is certainly necessary and has been lacking in the past.

At the same time the Chancellor announced that the 105% ceiling would, however, remain in force as regards the other financial institutions subject to it, until new arrangements could be worked out 'to secure from them an appropriate degree of restraint in their lending.' He also admitted that 'control of finance houses . . . presents special problems and a ceiling may be required there for a longer period while these are fully examined.'

Control Over Other Financial Institutions
During the late summer of 1967, the Bank of England privately circulated its proposals regarding the method of control for the other financial institutions operating in the UK*. These were submitted for consideration by the British overseas and Commonwealth banks, the foreign and American banks and the merchant banks. The form of control proposed was a version of 'special deposits', to be applied when the authorities wished for some restraint in the lending operations of these institutions.

Reimposition of Quantitative Control
However, with the devaluation of sterling in mid-November 1967, lending by banking institutions was once more placed under severe restraint. The Bank of England instructed that, apart from normal seasonal variations, there was to be no further growth in credit extended to the private sector, finance for exports alone being excepted.

---

* See 'The Banker', August 1967, page 657.

5. BASIC INADEQUACIES

So far, only the inadequacies of particular monetary weapons have been considered. But a broader look at the whole of monetary policy is also required to detect those areas where control through monetary methods is either inadequate or discontinuous. This involves examining the theoretical basis of monetary policy.

The place of monetary policy in the shape of things rests upon certain assumptions. The first of these. is that changes in the relationship between the supply of money and credit on the one hand and the volume of transactions on the other will have repercussions on the price level (this being the essence of what is known as the 'quantity theory') and on the general level of activity in the economy. The second basis of monetary policy rests on the question of interest rate responsiveness on the part of those either saving or making investment and other credit-financed spending decisions. Upward movements in interest rates are assumed to encourage saving, while discouraging investment and spending on consumer durables; with the converse applying when interest rates are lowered.

Regulation of Money and Credit
The first of these theoretical assumptions gives rise to concern in the operation of monetary policy with the supply of money and credit, the two sources of purchasing power. But considerable difficulty lies in the precise measurement of money supply and therefore in regulating it. Money supply consists of the number of monetary units and their velocity of circulation (that is, the number of times in a year each

unit performs the function of a means of payment). The units in money supply are coins, notes and, most important nowadays, bank deposits.

Near Money
This is the money supply strictly defined; but in addition there are categories of 'near' money in the form of balances which may be run down and thus significantly add to money supply. Such forms of near money include deposits at the Post Office and Trustee Savings banks, as well as those with building societies, hire purchase finance houses and local authorities. But, it would obviously be misleading to simply lump all these into money supply, since some of these balances represent genuine saving, rather than potential spending. The problem is of course to distinguish them. So, although the authorities can, if they want to, keep a close control over the rate at which notes and coin in circulation increase and on the cash base for the creation of bank deposits, there is no mechanism at present set up whereby they can control a rundown of near money balances at the Post Office savings banks, building societies etc.

Velocity of Circulation
The regulation of the money supply is also complicated by the possibility of variations in the velocity of circulation. This factor tends however not to work in the opposite direction from increases or decreases in the number of monetary units; but indeed operates to exaggerate such changes. The acceleration or deceleration effect of velocity is unfortunately not

forseeable in any precise terms; while velocity itself is exceedingly difficult to regulate.

Credit

The volume of credit is much more measurable and controllable: bank advances, commercial bills and hire purchase lending being the major forms it takes in this country. Part of this credit is, of course, included in the bank deposits part of money supply, since the banks employ just over half their deposits as advances to customers, with in addition a much smaller part in holding commercial bills.

The factor of credit must nevertheless be treated separately, for several reasons. Even in the case of the banks, the potential for credit expansion is different from that of deposits. By running down investments, the other major asset category, the banks can expand their advances at a faster rate than growth in deposits. Another reason for treating credit separately is that part of it comes from outside the commercial banks: from finance companies, whose deposits are one category of near money. Commercial bills are another form of credit, not included in money supply as it is usually defined. Apart from the commercial banks, these bills are also held by the acceptance houses (merchant banks) and the discount market.

Although the availability of credit is a more important determinant of purchasing power than the money supply itself, for most of the time there is no regulation exercised by the authorities over credit creation. Except when restrictive measures are imposed, there is no continuous control over bank lending. Similarly hire purchase finance houses are more or less left free to attract funds and pursue their lending operations. Indeed, the official policy of high short term rates during balance of payments deficit periods to discourage outflow of foreign funds also causes the hire purchase finance companies to attract additional loanable funds at a time when credit should be restrained rather than expanded.

Control Through Interest Rates
Saving
With interest rate responsiveness, not only is the degree, but also the direction, difficult to gauge with any certainty. National income calculations of 'saving' are more than usually tentative (and in any case include company retentions) so that it is difficult to prove any relationship between interest rate increase and a similar increase in the rate of saving. Conversely, lowering of interest rates is no deterrent to saving; indeed often the reverse—for, to guarantee a certain level of investment income, more may have to be saved.

Investment
The effect of interest rate changes upon investment may be similarly indeterminate. Much of business investment, being financed by retained earnings, is almost completely unresponsive to interest rate changes, except in cases where the concept of 'oppor-

tunity cost'[1] is applied. When the finance does have to be found from the capital market, even peak levels of long term interest rates do not deter businessmen from their investment plans, because they are at that stage generally too well advanced to be altered. Similarly, the greater cost of bank overdrafts is often viewed as just one of many cost increases, which in buoyant market conditions can readily be passed on to the consumer. In fact, the high points of investment in both stocks and fixed assets are invariably coincident with peak levels of interest rates, caused by many factors additional to the high level of demand for capital (see Table 5). In the reverse direction, it is not the lowness of interest rates that encourages businessmen to step up their investment, but rather expectations of improvement in the overall level of demand in the economy. Businessmen may be similarly unresponsive when the net cost of investment is reduced, either by government tax relief or by cash grant.

External Purposes

In the external sphere the attempt by a policy of high short term interest rates to discourage any outflow of foreign funds can only work initially. After that, if the deficit in our balance of payments is still continuing, loss of overseas confidence in our ability to

---

[1] The theory of 'opportunity cost' suggests that the real cost of using a factor of production, such as capital, is what it would have earned had it been employed elsewhere. In a period of high interest rates a more attractive alternative might be portfolio investment; and it is the return offered by this which can be used as a measure against which the expected return on direct investment may be compared.

TABLE 5

LEVELS OF INVESTMENT, BORROWING & INTEREST RATES

		1956	1957	1958	1959	1960	1961	1962	1963	1964	1965	1966
Stocks/Output Ratio (mid year)		96	98	102	95	94	100	102	98	96	98	98
Fixed Investment[1]	£m	854	947	922	867	1,021	1,239	1,168	1,044	1,216	1,401	1,456
New Capital Issues[2]	£m	158	262	175	145	212	310	183	173	234	267	423
Long Term Interest Rates[3]	%	4·73	4·98	4·98	4·82	5·42	6·20	5·98	5·58	6·03	6·42	6·80

[1] Manufacturing industry, at current prices.
[2] Manufacturing industry.
[3] Average gross flat yield on 2½% Consols.

55

support the pound will begin to outweigh the attractions of the high interest rates to be earned here. Where foreigners are still prepared to invest, they will do so only on a covered basis; so with increased demand for forward cover its cost will rise, reducing the effective differential between U.K. and overseas short term rates and therefore requiring a further increase in U.K. rates. The U.K's policy of high short term rates of interest to finance the early stages of the balance of payments deficit is always in danger of setting up an international interest rate war in which U.K. rates have to keep rising to stay above those overseas. This is the situation which the western world got itself into during 1966 and again in 1967.

Even if the interest rate weapon were to continue to be used for external purposes, the authorities' influence over the relevant U.K. short term rates is too indirect. Although the comparison in assessing the attractiveness of U.K. short term rates is no longer quite so much a matter of the U.K. as against the U.S. Treasury bill rate, nevertheless the authorities' main channel of influence continues to operate through the Treasury bill rate. More important nowadays is the comparison between the rates offered on three months' deposits with U.K. local authorities and hire purchase finance houses in relation to the rate on euro-dollars for a similar period.

The differential between local authority and finance house rates on the one hand and the Treasury bill and Bank rates on the other can vary quite considerably and therefore operation by the authorities on the latter is not a very exact way of achieving the required level of short term rates which compares favourably with those overseas, after taking into account the cost of forward cover. For example, in March 1965 the Treasury bill yield was 6·66%, whereas the rate offered for three months' deposits with local authorities was $7\frac{3}{4}\%$, so that the differential between these two was nearly $1\frac{1}{4}\%$. Towards the end of the same year this differential had narrowed to $\frac{3}{4}\%$; and in May 1966 it was as low as a $\frac{1}{2}\%$.

6. DISADVANTAGES OF MONETARY POLICY

The use of monetary policy has had certain disadvantages, not only for this country but also for the rest of the world. The internal deterrent effect of high interest rates has been mainly in the sphere of social investment, particularly housing, and this is one area the authorities least want to discourage. But for the rest of industry, high interest rates have been no deterrent during conditions of rampant boom. It has been the reduced availability, rather than any higher cost of credit, which has ultimately caused a reduction in demand.

High interest rates have also increased the burden of servicing, not only the national debt, but also the balances held in sterling by overseas residents (as well as any British government debt held by them). The former of course merely brings about a redistribution of income within the country; but the latter adds to our balance of payments 'invisible' outgoings. At the end of 1965 UK external sterling liabilities totalled nearly £6 thousand million; of which at least £1·5 thousand million was in interest-bearing short term investments, with another £1·2 thousand million in British government stocks. Non-residents' current and deposit accounts (only a combined figure being available) with UK banks (including merchant as well as clearing) totalled £1·9 thousand million. A very minimum figure nowadays for the estimated addition to our invisible debits would therefore be £27 million for every 1% increase in Bank rate, but the actual figure could be nearer £40 million. The estimate contained in the Radcliffe Report was £15 million.

The pursuance of monetary policy by way of high interest rates on the part of any one country, given the developed nature of the international short term capital market, inevitably has repercussions on other countries, and brings about a general upward movement in interest rates. Among the sufferers in this are the under-developed countries, whose need for capital is so great, but whose small export earnings are inadequate to cover high loan servicing charges.

These disadvantages of high interest rates, resulting from excessive reliance on monetary policy, may cause the authorities to revise the balance of monetary and fiscal measures in controlling the economy. The Labour party has a traditional dislike of high interest rates and the immediate post-war Labour government made little use of monetary weapons, managing to retain the low level of interest rates begun in the 'thirties.

Interest Rate Disarmament
Towards the end of January 1967 the British Chancellor of the Exchequer convened a 'Chequers' conference to try to achieve 'a measure of international disarmament in the present level of interest rates'. This was attended by ministers from France, Italy, United States and Western Germany, who agreed to co-operate to bring down the level of interest rates. This aspiration was translated into action during the following three months by reductions in the central bank discount rates (Bank rate) in Britain, Germany, USA and other financial centres. However, from the

early summer onwards events forced interest rates to rise once again.

PART THREE

PRICES AND INCOMES BOARD: Report on Bank Charges

REPORT ON BANK CHARGES[1]

Scope of Enquiry

A partial attempt at setting in train the much needed reconsideration of monetary policy was made in 1967 by the National Board for Prices and Incomes, using as a vehicle for this the reference made to it regarding bank charges. The terms of enquiry, in fact, specifically excluded monetary policy " . . . It is not intended that the Board should concern itself with questions of monetary policy such as Bank Rate and the general level of interest rates."[2] Nevertheless, the Prices and Incomes Board decided to interpret this " . . . as meaning that we should not comment on the way in which monetary policy has been conducted or on the general level at which Bank Rate has been held . . . In so far, however, as we recommend changes in the system of bank charges, such changes are likely to have considerable implications for the techniques of monetary control. We have accordingly thought it consistent with our terms of reference to indicate what these implications might be and what possibilities by way of offsetting action might be open to the authorities".[3]

Since, however, the Board did decide to interpret its brief fairly broadly, despite having been 'warned off' from doing so, its Report does provide an opportunity to consider some further 'official' utterances on the subject of monetary policy. The more mundane aspects that the Board *was* asked to examine are not

---

[1] National Board for Prices and Incomes: Report No. 34, 'Bank Charges' Cmnd. 3292. HMSO.

[2] ibid, page 3, para. 1.

[3] ibid, page 7, para. 3.

of interest in the context of this study. Nor are we concerned with the strictly domestic matters of opening hours or even the wider issue of the publication of the banks' true profits. Nor need we dwell too much upon those matters which would certainly be of interest in any study of monopoly and restrictive practices.

Although, by and large, the banking community reacted unfavourably to the PIB Report[1], it is clear from a reading of it that the Board was basically on the side of the banks. Its theme throughout was that the banks should recapture the ground lost to the other financial institutions and the Board believed that monetary policy should evolve to enable them to do so.

Bank Deposit Growth
The opening part of the Report contained a table showing how growth of bank deposits had been outstripped by those of the other financial institutions[2] and how it even failed to keep pace with growth in GNP. But it should be noted that the period selected began with deposits at a high level during an expansion period (1959) and ended at a time (1965) when advances, and therefore deposits, were under restraint. There is therefore a compression effect, which partly

---

[1] They did however respond with some alacrity to the PIB's revelation: 'The Bank of England and the Treasury have made it plain to us that they would not obstruct some further amalgamations if the banks were willing to contemplate such a development . . . ' (page 53, para 154).

[2] Post Office & Trustee Savings banks, building societies, overseas banks and accepting houses, hire purchase companies.

explains the low growth rate of bank deposits. And it cannot be argued that the 1965 restraint was a factor entirely common to all the financial institutions included in the comparison—for some of them managed to evade this restraint (at least during 1965) while many of the others were not subject to it all. Furthermore, such comparisons spread over a period of years, while seeking to present a fair average, mislead by obscuring the expansionist years during which growth in certain areas in money and credit supply is in fact excessive and contributes therefore to inflationary pressures. It is what happens in these years, rather than over a six year period, which is of vital importance (as can be seen from Table 3 on page 42, where the growth rate of bank cash can, because of the constant 8% ratio, be equated with the overall growth rate of bank deposits). The table in the PIB Report therefore tends to have the unfortunate effect of seeming to confirm the banks in their customary rejection of any responsibility for causing excess inflationary pressures by their lending and therefore of any need for the authorities to control the growth rate of bank deposits.

Banking Competition

As has already been said, the PIB was anxious that the banks should recover their lost ground. Its Report suggested that they could do so by becoming more competitive, abandoning their cartel arrangements regarding rates charged for advances and given for deposits, and by being more open about their system for levying bank charges on customers. Freeing their rates would also give them flexibility to offer varying rates according to length of time deposit.

The Report noted that there were lending areas, such as instalment loans and house mortgages, included in banking proper in many other countries, which British banks had been reluctant to mix with their normal banking operations, preferring instead to operate such activities through wholly or partly owned subsidiaries or else not to engage in them at all. Apart from improving competitiveness, were the banks to put aside these inhibitions, the Board felt that substantial economies from integration could be reaped.

The significance of all this from the point of view of monetary policy was that since the banks had always been much more readily subjected to monetary control, the greater the proportion of total money and credit within their creation the easier would be the authorities' task. It should be noted that Exchequer financing is also assisted, for banks invest in government bills and bonds to a much greater extent. than naturally do either building societies or finance companies.

Monetary Theory
In the context of discussing the impact on banks of competition from other financial institutions, the PIB Report made some tantalisingly brief observations on points of monetary theory.[1] It did so by way

---

[1] National Board for Prices and Incomes: Report No. 34. 'Bank Charges' Cmnd. 3292. HMSO, page 29, paras 58–59.

of questioning two pieces of rationalisation which had been developed in recent years to provide solace for the banks.

Loss of Deposits
It had been argued by the rationalisers that the growth of these other deposit-taking institutions, by the very nature of our monetary processes, could not in fact rob the banks of deposits. Money lent to building societies or finance companies would eventually find its way into somebody's bank account. This, the PIB argued, was not necessarily true. The banks did not always recapture money lost through cheques drawn upon them to make deposits with other institutions. Money 'banked' with bodies like the Post Office and Trustee Savings Banks went directly to the government by their uptake of gilt-edged securities. Much more important, this caused a reduction in bankers' balances at the Bank of England and thus a contraction of the cash base upon which bank deposits could be created. The PIB could, however, have gone further in tracing the course of events, as indeed it did in its second example. Staying for a moment with the first, it can be argued that if the proceeds of 'small savings' are used to finance investment in the public sector, this expenditure, by generating national income, would also create bank deposits.

The second example of loss of deposits by the banks to competing financial institutions was the case of hire purchase companies. Here the chain of reasoning was much longer. Money transferred from a bank account to a finance company caused such an increase in lending that eventually the adverse effects on the balance of payments forced the authorities to take offsetting action by open market sales of securities (but as we saw earlier, because of the weak state of the gilt-edged market, this is just what they often find themselves unable to do). Such open market sales, the Board pointed out, would reduce the banking system's reserves. That they did over the long run would again depend on what the government did with the proceeds.

All this is, of course, is an area of monetary theory which offers even greater than usual scope for endless discussion, chiefly because in the circulation of money and credit the chain itself is endless. But some further points could perhaps have been made by the PIB Report in contesting the view that banks cannot lose deposits. Small cash deposits are the stuff that the overall banking system's deposit growth is made of and these are substantially provided by the private individual. Industrial and commercial firms tend in the main to be net borrowers from the banking system, rather than depositors. Thus, the more the small depositor is lured away from the banking system, by the offer of a better return elsewhere, the less of the raw material for lending and deposit creation is available to the banks.

Furthermore, the channels along which the non-bank financial institutions inject money may be areas where bank accounts are less used. Deposits made with hire purchase companies eventually find their way into the pay packets of workers in the motor industry. Soon afterwards, of course, this may well go into the tills and bank accounts of local shop-keepers. But the velocity of circulation of bank deposits will have been less and more cash will probably have leaked out of the banking system, to be held by the public; whereas if the deposit had been made in the first instance with a bank it would have been lent to a firm whose payments would have been very largely made by cheque, including its salary payments, and thus into other bank accounts. Although, therefore, money deposited with the non-banking institutions may at some stage find its way into bank accounts, the number of banking transactions involved in the circulation of this money and credit will be fewer, and it is this opportunity to handle people's money which the banking system is losing.

Creation of Money and Credit

Another aspect of monetary doctrine touched upon by the Report was the question of: Just how 'different' are banks in their capacity to create money and credit? The Board felt that they were not as completely different as is sometimes represented by monetary theorists. The Report suggested that other financial institutions 'share with the banks some ability (albeit an inferior one) to 'create credit' in the sense that an extension of their lending is liable to give rise to an increase in income and saving; part of this increased saving will be placed afresh with these

institutions, thus further raising their lending power'.[1]
All this is really saying is that hire purchase lending, for
example, turns savings back into spending (and so
increases the propensity to consume) in a way that is
particularly national income generative. Out of this
larger income there will certainly be more saving, part
of which will be deposited with the institutions
extending the credit in the first place.

These various asides on monetary theory contained
in the Report might be regarded by some as being so
superficial as to be hardly worth making. But, in
fairness, it should be recognised that the Board's
intention was probably more to raise the issues,
rather than explore them conclusively, in the hope
that this might be done elsewhere.

Reserve and Liquidity Ratios
The authors of the PIB Report felt that consideration
could be given by the authorities to making some
reduction in the requirements regarding the banks'
cash and liquidity ratios.[2] At the same time, they
urged that official conventions with regard to reserves
and liquidity should be enforced on other deposit-
taking financial institutions; including a recommended
ratio of liquid assets to deposit liabilities and a laid
down ratio of capital and reserves to borrowed funds.[3]
Among the advantages of doing so would be greater
assurance of liquidity and solvency, and perhaps

---

[1] National Board for Prices and Incomes: Report No. 34. 'Bank Charges'
Cmnd. 3292. HMSO, page 12, para. 15.

[2] ibid, page 32, para. 69.

[3] ibid.

better protection for depositors. It would also provide continuous instruments of monetary control in areas where they had so far been lacking. These proposals, including some relaxation of the bank's ratios, would also make for competition on a more equal footing between the banks and the other institutions.[1]

Interest Rates
The report made no comment on the authorities' use of the interest rate weapon. Admittedly, they were expressly asked not to; but this need not have been a hindrance if they had felt strongly on the subject. They touched on high interest rates only by way of noting their effect of providing the banks with an additional element of profit: while earnings on bank assets are geared to interest rates, just over half their deposits are lodged on an interest-free basis, the cost of services given in return not being affected by the level of interest rates. Instead of dwelling on this as just another of the inequitable features of a policy of high interest rates, the Report merely considered the possibility of some sort of equalising action by the authorities in the form of a special levy on bank profits in the years of high Bank rate, with a rebate being given in the years when Bank rate was low.[2]

Many of the Report's proposals entailed increased flexibility of interest rates, through untying them from collective agreement based upon Bank rate and thereby enabling greater competition between financial institutions in the winning of deposits. This, the

---

[1] ibid, page 32, para. 70.

[2] ibid, page 25, para. 46.

Board argued,[1] would not necessarily impair the authorities' power of monetary control, since it left unaffected the major weapons of open market operations, special deposits and reserve ratios for influencing the level of bank lending. This would seem pretty much to ignore the interest rate weapon (perhaps rightly) and particularly control over the Treasury bill rate through the fixing of 'call money' rates on the basis of Bank rate.

The Board also examined the question of whether this greater flexibility would make for higher interest rates.[2] On the whole it thought not. If there did appear any danger of a bidding up of rates, it suggested that the authorities could always impose maximum rates to be paid on deposits[3]—shades of Regulation Q![4] All this is not very convincing. A result of this flexibility and competition would very likely be to unleash domestically the same sort of interest rate war that has waged internationally in recent years. Since overdrafts in this country are already given on softer terms, by comparison with term loans in other countries, there would be less scope for holding down lending rates by absorbing upward movements of deposit rates in profit margins—although the PIB apparently felt that they could to some extent be offset by cost reduction.[5] One might remark that,

[1] ibid, page 33, para. 75.
[2] ibid, page 34, para. 80.
[3] ibid, page 61, para. 185.
[4] This is the regulation whereby the US Federal Reserve system lays down the maximum rates of interest that member banks may pay on deposits.
[5] PIB Report, page 35, para. 80.

from an overall monetary control point of view, it might in fact not be a bad thing to have more expensive overdrafts, as this would restrain excessive over-utilisation of credit.

Discount Market
As it did in the Radcliffe Report, the question of the justification of the existence of the discount market once more came under scrutiny. The PIB acknowledged that a study of the practices of the discount houses would clearly be outside its terms of reference. It therefore contented itself with the observation: 'There would have been no case for arrangements specially designed to keep the discount houses in being if the clearing banks had themselves developed the functions discharged by the discount houses.'[1] The Board could see no objection at all to the Bank of England acting directly as a lender of last resort to the clearing banks, as it noted was the practice in many other countries.[2] The discount market thus gets slightly rougher treatment from the PIB than that given it by the Radcliffe Committee, which rather inconclusively remarked: 'It would not be beyond human ingenuity to replace the work of the discount houses; but they are there, they are doing the work effectively, and they are doing it at a trifling cost in terms of labour and other real resources.'[3]

---

[1] National Board for Prices and Incomes: Report No. 34. 'Bank Charges' Cmnd. 3292. HMSO, page 39, para. 96.

[2] In America, for example, the member banks borrow reserves from the Federal Reserve bank at the latter's discount window.

[3] Radcliffe Report, page 64, para. 180.

The cost to society of having a discount market, as the PIB Report noted, is the higher rate of interest that has to be paid on bills and bonds to cover the expenses of running the discount houses and provide them with a profit. The published profits of the twelve discount houses in 1966 added up to around £4 million, there being in addition undisclosed transfers to reserves. No information is available on the discount houses' costs of operation, but tax paid by them has been deducted from the profit figure.

Conclusion
These then are the points of monetary policy touched upon in the PIB Report. On the subject that it was asked to look into, namely bank charges, the Report concluded that the banks' charges and commissions could not be regarded as being too high: they had encountered little complaint about them from the general public. The Board did, however, recommend that greater publicity should be given by the banks as to their method of arriving at charges. It concluded that the excessive profits earned and dividends paid out by the banks had resulted rather from the endowment element of high levels of Bank rate, together with agreement between the banks as to interest rates charged and paid.

Commercial Institutions or Public Utilities?
Despite the somewhat indignant reception accorded the Report by the clearing banks, they may in retrospect be regarded as being treated comparatively gently. It could have been worse. There is much

touched upon in the Report that might quite properly have been regarded as being within the sphere of restrictive practices. And any other body might not have been quite so obliging, as the Board was, in adopting as a basic assumption that the banks must necessarily continue as 'commercial institutions'.[1] There is much in their character, and indeed in the way they have come to do business, which could equally qualify the banks to be regarded as being more akin to 'public utilities'. Certainly, in providing a major part of the nation's money supply, their activity is very 'basic' to the working of the economy— even more so than in say the case of the steel industry. The services provided by the banks are very similar; they all largely deal in the same raw material and finished product. The price they pay and charge for money is the same. The banks were found to have been earning in recent years excessive profits,[2] part of which they have used in a needless proliferation of premises. In this way, it would not have been difficult for anyone so minded to have built up a case for taking as a basic assumption that the more natural home of the banks is in the public, rather than the private, sector.

---

[1] This was stressed again by Mr. Aubrey Jones in an article in the 'Bankers' Magazine', August 1967.

[2] This giving rise to what Mr. Aubrey Jones described in his article as 'political vulnerability'.

PART IV

Reform of Monetary Policy

When describing the monetary techniques available to the authorities, it was seen how in practice they frequently fell short of maximum effectiveness; and in doing so created certain dangers. Because of this, consideration must be given, not only to the reform of monetary policy, but also in certain areas to abandoning its use altogether. The Prices and Incomes Board Report gave some pointers on this, but there were naturally many aspects it left untouched.

1. EXTERNAL ASPECTS

In assessing the need for change, the use of monetary policy for external purposes will be examined first, since it is difficulties in Britain's balance of payments that generally force the authorities to institute monetary action by bringing about a rise in short term interest rates.

Non-sustainable Elements

At the time, this is usually represented as simply a precaution to safeguard the reserves against purely speculative short term capital outward movements, as well as any attempted rundown of sterling balances. However, as indeed happened in the first half of 1964, the authorities' interest rate policy does more than this: it positively attracts short term capital and encourages further build-up of sterling balances.[1] In this way a balance of payments deficit can be covered up, at least as far as being revealed in the reserves is concerned. Such a policy can, of course, succeed only for a certain time; sooner or later the truth will out and the outflow will be all the greater, as a result of funds having been attracted in the first place. The Report of Working Party No. 3.[2] drew attention to the purely temporary relief to be obtained from attracting short-term capital inflows:

'A situation of apparent balance defined in terms of official reserves may, however, be dependent upon elements which are not likely to be sustainable, and in particular on capital flows (either long term or short) whose continuance cannot be relied on. In determining the need for action, countries should clearly take account of such non-sustainable elements . . . '

(Page 11, para 18.)

Disadvantages of High Interest Rates
Thus, there is an element of danger, as well as deception, in this use of the monetary weapon. There

---

[1] After taking into account a positive balancing item of £54 million, the basic payments deficit in the first half of 1964 was £314 million; but this was more than covered by a build-up of sterling balances to the extent of £169 million and an inflow of short term capital of £109 million, so that in fact there was a small rise in our reserves.

[2] 'The Balance of Payments Adjustment Process', a report by Working Party No. 3 of the Economic Policy Committee of the Organisation for Economic Co-operation and Development—August 1966.

are also other disadvantages. Action by the British authorities may set off a rise in the level of world interest rates. Once again, Working Party No. 3. may be quoted. Referring to the effect of countries' monetary policies on international capital transactions the Report said ' . . . this is a field where some measure of international co-operation is important. Without such a measure of co-operation there may be a danger of inappropriate international levels of interest rates . . . ' (page 22, para 50).

As already noted, high UK short term rates also increase the burden of externally held debt, since much of this is short-dated stocks and bills. And as long as the deficit is not reflected in our reserves there will be a tendency to delay taking remedial action; high interest rates in themselves being more masking than corrective. The penalty effect of high interest rates as far as the internal economy is concerned tends to be concentrated in areas of social investment, particularly housing.

It would therefore be better all round if this aspect of monetary policy were to be abandoned altogether. It is the move by Britain into deficit that is likely to cause a withdrawal of foreign privately owned funds, and not any irrational change of psychology on the part of so called 'speculators'. The danger of withdrawal can be better averted by correcting the deficit, than by putting up interest rates, which only tends to attract speculative funds.

Official Attitudes

In this, as in other areas, there is misconception. 'Hot money' is deplored and the gnomes of Zurich are accused of selling sterling short. But the authorities bring in the hot money in the first place by their interest rate policy. The jacking-up of interest rates is of course always represented, not as attracting hot money in, but as keeping it from flowing out. As a short term method of financing the balance of payments deficit, it is justified on the grounds that it merely offsets speculative 'leads and lags' in payments. Furthermore, Bank rate action, it is believed, shows the foreigner that the British government is determined to curb inflationary excesses. It is also argued that, with convertibility and our particular vulnerability to short term disequilibrating movements arising from our large sterling balance liabilities, the authorities have no alternative but to resort to such practices. The effect achieved, however, is not simply restricted to sterling balances but also embraces inflows of speculative short term funds, chiefly in the form of euro-dollars. These the authorities could seek to discourage if they wanted to.

Discouraging 'Hot Money'

Plenty of other countries in Europe take steps to keep out hot money,[1] wisely denying themselves this method of covering up payments deficits. Of course, in the case of many of these countries, the relatively undeveloped nature of their short-term capital markets narrows the investment opportunities available to foreign funds; and this to some extent also makes official regulation easier. Even so, the great variety of controls imposed by European countries testifies to the existence of a need, coupled with a willingness, to repel 'hot money' inflows. Deposits received by European banks from abroad are often subject to physical limitation or to special reserve requirements. Acceptance of foreign deposits by banks in some countries reduces their rediscounting privilege at the central bank. Foreigners may not even be allowed to hold short-term government securities and banks forbidden to pay interest on foreign-owned time deposits. Foreign borrowing by a country's nationals may be discouraged or even prohibited. Many European central banks intervene in the foreign exchange market by offering low cost covered swaps into other currencies, thereby encouraging the re-routing abroad of any foreign funds which may happen to have come in uninvited.

All this is in striking contrast with practice in this country, where often the express purpose of intervention in the forward market[2] is to encourage short-term capital inflow by keeping down the cost of cover. Overall, the continentals have tended to be more active in taking steps to keep out 'hot money'; while we, and the Americans, in ostensibly seeking to discourage short-term capital outflows, have not been averse to encouraging inflows. The unwillingness of

---

[1] See Thirty-sixth Annual Report of Bank for International Settlements, June 1966, pages 46-47.

[2] Since the November 1967 devaluation such intervention seems to have been abandoned.

the UK authorities to exercise control to keep out 'hot money' is sometimes attributed to a desire not to impair the functioning of London as an international financial centre, and the accompanying very welcome 'invisible' earnings. However, the re-routing action of the sort which is taken in other countries, while keeping out hot money on a 'net' basis, does nothing to diminish the international banking function, but indeed adds to it.[1]

Reserves and Money Supply
Gold Standard Automaticity

Ever since Britain left the gold standard in 1931 there has been an absence of any link between the state of our reserves and the internal money supply. The existence of this connection under the gold standard brought into play certain automatic corrective mechanisms to deal with deficits and surpluses in the balance of payments. The volume of internal money supply was determined by the stock of gold. When an adverse balance of trade developed, the country's currency became in excess supply in the foreign exchange market and its exchange rate therefore dropped to the lower gold point, at which it became cheaper for those requiring foreign currencies to send gold abroad to buy them. This drain of gold from the deficit country caused its internal monetary supply to contract. Reduction in money supply, in the face of a constant production of goods and services, in turn caused prices to fall. The country's goods became competitive in world markets, with imports dearer by

<hr>

[1]This is pointed out by Mr. P.M. Oppenheimer in an article, 'Short-term Capital Flows' in 'The Banker' of August 1967, page 674.

comparison, and this expansion of exports and discouragement of imports corrected the adverse balance of trade.

The corrective mechanism was in the opposite direction when the country had a balance of trade surplus. Scarcity of its currency in the foreign exchange market drove its exchange rate to the upper gold point, at which foreigners found it cheaper to ship gold to the country to buy its currency, rather than buy in the foreign exchange market. This inflow of gold expanded the domestic money supply, setting in train a rise in prices, which discouraged exports and encouraged imports.

There were in practice difficulties hindering the perfect operation of this theoretically self-correcting system. Even where countries observed the rules of the gold standard, allowing their domestic money supply to reflect movement in their reserves, and did not resort to artificial measures to influence imports and exports, the existence of certain rigidities in prices and wages tended to cause production, rather than prices, to fall. As a result unemployment would be widespread, while exports remained uncompetitive.

Modern Missing Link
Today, not only have we abandoned the automatic pilot, but some aspects of our modern policy give rise to greater divergence between internal and external objectives. There is certainly no longer any formal link between the state of our gold reserves and the

size of our internal money supply. If we lose gold nowadays the money supply need not necessarily be contracted.

It is true that in drawing gold or foreign currencies from the Exchange Equalisation Account, to enable traders to pay for the excess of imports over exports, the commercial banks have their balances at the Bank of England debited, as well as their own deposits reduced by the sterling equivalent of the foreign currency supplied to importers.[1] The debiting of their balances at the Bank of England reduces bank cash, but this can be made good by running down liquid assets, which in any case are now at a higher percentage level due to the contraction in total bank deposits. These liquid assets released by the banks may be taken up by the Exchange Equalisation Account, which now has a larger sterling content. But the amount of liquid assets required to be sold by the banks to compensate for the cash loss will bring the liquidity ratio down to a lower level than before. Thus the lasting effects of the payments deficit upon the banking system will be a reduction in deposits and a lower liquidity ratio. However, these effects may very well be completely swamped by the authorities' open market purchases of securities, and, even more so, by an increase in government spending relative to taxation.

If the foreigner is prepared to accept payment in

---

[1] See Professor Sayers' 'Modern Banking' (Oxford University Press) 6th Edition, pages 146-151.

the form of a sterling bank balance, then there is a shift in ownership of bank deposits from resident to non-resident. But there is no reduction in total deposits and therefore no reduction in money supply. Nor, really, does the transfer of ownership of deposits involve a reduction in domestic purchasing power, since the externally owned deposits are on the liabilities side of the balance sheet and may be employed on the assets side in loans to UK residents. These foreign-owned deposits may be extinguished if they are used to buy UK exports or exchanged for gold or foreign currencies. If either of these happens, money supply will be reduced.

When non-resident sterling balances are employed in the euro-sterling market they remain within the UK money supply and can only be extinguished in the manner described in the previous paragraph. Euro-sterling may indeed be borrowed by UK financial institutions and used to extend, for example, hire purchase credit. This would, of course, merely involve a shift of ownership of bank deposits in the UK from non-residents temporarily back to the residents' category, although the financial institution borrowing the euro-sterling to lend to the finance company will also have enlarged its deposits.

This brings us to another paradox of modern monetary practice. When the authorities, during a period of payments deficit, pursue a policy of high short term interest rates, the rate offered, for example by finance companies on three months' deposits, is increased. As a result, savings are attracted from home and abroad, and diverted (via hire purchase lending) back to consumption. This increases the volume of credit available for the purchase of consumer durables and the result is likely to be inflationary, making the balance of trade position worse. Other key short term rates are those offered on deposits placed with local authorities. When these rise, the overseas funds they attract enable local authorities to indulge in a higher level of both current and capital spending, thereby putting additional demand pressure upon resources, already scarce enough in an overfully employed economy.

2. INTERNAL USES

In all the talk about national planning and overall growth rates for the economy, less has been said about the problem of ensuring that the supply of the means of payment keeps in line with the growth of goods and services. Perhaps this is because it has been assumed that this has for long been a continuing responsibility of monetary policy. If so, then our rate of inflation suggests that this responsibility has been less than adequately fulfilled. Considering the extent to which many sectors of our economy are now closely regulated, it is surprising that such an important matter as the supply of money and credit is still on a laissez-faire basis: to result from the pursuit of self-interest by the major financial institutions.

As we have seen, the major elements in money and credit are: notes and coins, bank deposits, 'near money' balances, bank advances and hire purchase lending. A consideration of monetary policy reform involves examining better ways of controlling these elements.

Money Supply

Over recent years the rate at which notes and coins have increased has corresponded fairly closely to that of GNP (the notable exception being in 1965). At first sight, the official view[1] on this is somewhat perplexing: 'that the government's function in issuing notes is simply the passive one of ensuring that sufficient notes are available for the practical conveni-

---

[1] As reported in the Radcliffe Report, para. 348.

ence of the public'. This apparently lackadaisical attitude becomes less worrying, however when it is remembered that it is the banks' *cash* position which is the important determinant of the growth potential for bank deposits. And bank cash is not simply a matter of the volume of notes and coin in circulation: it is made up not only of the banks' 'till money' but also their accounts in the Banking Department of the Bank of England (these being known as 'Bankers' Balances'). The actual physical supply of notes and coinage merely derives from what happens to these Balances.

Movements in the overall size of Bankers' Balances reflect changes in the flow of funds between the public (i.e. government) and private sectors; this flow itself depending upon variations in government spending relative to taxation, and also on whether the authorities are net sellers or purchasers of their own securities. The second of these is in the sphere of monetary policy and is also probably the more readily controllable of the two. Despite this, the authorities have frequently felt inhibited from pursuing open market operations for fear of causing disorderly conditions in the gilt-edged market, with repercussions on the strength of sterling in the foreign exchange markets. Part of this reluctance has also been based on the belief (largely wishful thinking) that a policy of high short term rates can be pursued without having at the same time high long term rates, with all the penalties this entails for investment, both social and manufacturing.

Overriding Fiscal Influence

The dominant determinant of Bankers' Balances is not monetary but fiscal policy. Government expenditure and taxation is all important in regulating Bankers' Balances, and therefore the cash base for the creation of the largest element in our money supply, namely bank deposits. Fiscal action is however more likely to lose a government popularity; so that there is a political preference for using monetary means wherever possible. It is here that the real weakness in control over money and credit lies. Although it has long been fashionable to deride the very idea of 'balancing the budget', nevertheless more attention could be paid to the repercussions of fiscal policy on the cash base of the banking system. This is admittedly an area of difficulty, since tax changes occur only once or twice a year; while government spending is not always readily re-phased. Open-market operations provide an instrument of greater continuity and precision. But, as in the case of trying to curb consumption by encouraging saving, it is not always easy to get the public to buy gilt-edged stocks. The prevailing climate is generally against this: good company profits make equities attractive and this, coupled with a high rate of inflation, tends to reduce the appeal of National Savings and government stocks. Again, this underlines the need for fiscal action to back up monetary techniques.

Near Money Balances

Despite official attempts to restrict money supply, the

public, if they are really determined to spend, can obtain purchasing power by running down near money balances. This raises the question of whether the authorities can do anything to prevent this. Higher interest rates paid on these balances may persuade some holders to desist from spending. But again there may be a conflict of official policy; for in the case of building societies the government has more often sought to restrain the raising of the reward to investors, with the result that balances with building societies have been run down and not always reinvested elsewhere.

Steps could also be taken to make these near money balances less liquid: to reverse the trend of recent years towards greater liquidity, through informal relaxation of notice of withdrawal requirements. With official prompting, notice could be more strictly enforced to give such balances more the character of genuine saving, rather than potential spending.

Credit Control

The most volatile element in purchasing power is credit, the availability of which is dependent upon the saver's abstinence. As borrowed purchasing power, credit inevitably represents a channelling back of savings to consumption and has therefore inflationary potential. The volume of credit can over a period of months expand quite dramatically, pushing the price level up with it. In the case of bank lending, this occurs because the potential for bank advances is not limited to the growth rate in deposits, but can exceed this by the realisation of investments. When restrictions are off, hire purchase lending similarly expands quite unchecked, with no reference to any overall growth rate of the economy. This absence of any continuous official control over credit means that when restriction eventually does have to be imposed it is inevitably disruptive and naturally resented by those who, up till then, have pursued their operations unguided by the authorities.

Not that there is any lack of devices for control over credit; they are in fact numerous, although often uncertain in their effect. In the case of hire purchase, the availability of this form of credit may be varied by altering the length of the repayment period, the size of the minimum deposit, or the interest rate charged. To this has been added in recent years the same sort of quantitative limit as has been applied to clearing and merchant bank lending, either by way of advances or by commercial bills. The clearing banks themselves have been 'requested' to favour certain types of borrower more than others; while deposits have been denied employment as advances by being taken for special deposits.

Alternatives to Quantitative Limit
The most effective of these controls over credit in recent years was undoubtedly the imposition of the 5% quantitative limit, until deflation naturally reduced the public appetite for advances. The quantitative limit was, however, much resented by bankers as being arbitrary; having no reference to the rate at

91

H

which deposits were being acquired and treating no more kindly those who had in fact heeded the earlier requests for restraint. To take into account these valid objections, perhaps a better method of controlling advances growth would be for the authorities to designate a maximum percentage of deposits which could be employed as advances; and it would probably be wise to include commercial bill holdings under this as well. An alternative way of restraining the additional impetus to advances growth, which comes from the running down by the banks of their holdings of gilt-edged securities, would be to postulate a minimum percentage for the investment category. This would also assist in Exchequer financing. These maximum and minimum percentages could be variable.

Dearer Borrowing
The public's appetite for advances could of course be lessened by making the overdraft a more expensive form of credit. The banks have tended to lend at a much cheaper rate than other financial institutions, both here and abroad. Interest is charged only on what has been actually borrowed, and not on the total credit facility. The cost of advances has been further reduced by the tax relief extended to the borrower in respect of the interest paid on his overdraft. This concession has helped to make nonsense of any idea of a deterrent effect of the interest rate weapon.

One reason the banks have been able to lend so

cheaply is, of course, that they obtain 60% of their funds on an interest-free basis, providing instead certain services, particularly the cheque facility. This non-payment of interest on current accounts dates only from 1945, at which time interest rates were in any case very low. In recent years, when the banks have been able to earn 8% to 9% on advances, there has been less justification for withholding interest payment on current accounts and thus favouring the spenders rather than the holders of balances.

Hire Purchase
Controlling the volume of hire purchase debt is probably more difficult. At certain levels, variation in the initial deposit and repayment period has little influence on the demand for the hire purchase facility, as witness the ineffectiveness of the progressive tightening of hire purchase terms during the twelve months up to July 1966 (see Table 6). It was only after this date that the outstanding hire purchase debt really fell, despite the fact that lending had been subject to a 105% ceiling over March 1965. Since hire purchase is particularly associated with passenger car demand, the many fiscal means of operating on the latter could also be effective in governing the volume of hire purchase credit.

Cash and Liquidity Ratios

Returning to banking proper, flexibility in cash and liquidity ratios has so far in this country been one way only; although in other countries such ratios are moved up, as well as down. The adoption of this

TABLE 6

HIRE PURCHASE RESTRICTIONS

	Total Hire Purchase Debt Outstanding £ million	
3rd June 1965: minimum deposit on cars went up from 20% to 25%; on electrical goods (except cookers) from 10% to 15%; on bedding, furniture, cookers and water heaters the minimum deposit remained unchanged at 10%.	1329 1343 1354	1965 May June July
27th July 1965: another tightening up on hire purchase: this time by reducing the repayment period from 36 to 30 months, except in the case of furniture, cookers and water heaters.	1343 1354 1358	1965 June July August
8th February 1966: a reduction in the hire purchase repayment period; coming down in the case of most goods from 30 to 24 months. On goods where the initial deposit had been 15% this was now raised to 25%; on furniture it went up from 10% to 15%. In the case of cars, the repayment period only came down to 27 months, with no alteration in the initial deposit.	1374 1367 1357	1966 January February March
20th July 1966: hire purchase minimum deposits were raised from 25% to 40% on cars, with the repayment period being shortened to 24 months; down-payments on furniture were increased from 15% to 20%; and on domestic appliances from 25% to 33⅓%.	1363 1362 1335	1966 June July August

94

practice in Britain would make the monetary steering of the economy much more direct and would also enable some reduction in the multiplicity of monetary weapons. For example, the banks' response to action by the authorities to contract the cash base could be made much more immediate by increasing the cash ratio, without first having to bring the banks nearer to their minimum liquidity ratio by funding and special deposits. The liquidity ratio itself might even be forgotten about, at least as far as monetary policy is concerned. After all, the monetary authorities in many other countries seem to manage quite successfully with only a cash reserve ratio, although it should be noted that in such cases the ratio is variable.

Supply of Liquid Assets.
There could also be a greater degree of official abandonment of the significance that has been traditionally attached by the authorities in their monetary control to the supply of liquid assets to the banking system. It was earlier indicated how a very substantial contraction in the supply of Treasury bills during the fiscal year 1964/5 was nevertheless rendered futile by a ready substitution of holdings of commercial bills by the banks in their liquid assets category. The steps that had subsequently to be taken to bring commercial bill creation under control and limit their acceptability as security for assistance given to the discount market by the central bank add too much to the complexity of monetary policy. Furthermore, it still in any case leaves too many other liquid asset

alternatives available to the banks for the volume of Treasury bills to be a significant limiting factor in restricting growth of bank deposits.

Interest Rates

We return now to the question of the effectiveness of control over short term rates through the authorities' influence on the Treasury bill rate, supposing that the interest rate weapon is still going to be used. The more important key short term rates today are those offered on three months' deposits by local authorities and finance companies. But, since the extent to which these exceed bill rate can vary (between $\frac{1}{2}\%$ and $1\frac{3}{8}\%$) the precise level of UK rates required (vis-à-vis those overseas) might be more readily obtained by operating on these rates directly. In the case of local authorities this could be done by varying the extent to which financial assistance was available from the Exchequer, through the Public Works Loan Board and other sources; and also the extent to which, and the terms on which, the local authorities 'fund'. Official directives regarding advances and acceptances by banks and discount houses to finance companies would influence the extent to which the latter depended upon deposits and therefore the rate they offered. Upon finance houses, the government could bring to bear the same pressure it occasionally attempts to exert on building societies.

If its rate becomes less important, so also does the Treasury bill, as well as indeed Bank rate. This also brings into question the continued need for the ritual

96

of the weekly tender and for 'front' and 'back door' assistance; and indeed the existence of the discount market itself. Since the nationalisation of the Bank of England formally gave it power over the banks, there is no longer any reason, as the Prices and Incomes Board recognised, why the contact between the Bank and the clearing banks for adjustment of the cash position should not be direct.

Conclusions

Certain very broad conclusions emerge from what has been said above. Since there are no longer pretensions about Britain being an uncontrolled economy, there is less need to continue to favour mechanisms which make use of natural market forces. There could therefore be a reduced reliance on monetary policy; much of it being in any case very uncertain as regards effectiveness, and valuable time is often lost in finding this out.

Continuous Control Over Money and Credit

A weeding out of the tangle of monetary techniques is also desirable. The use of short term interest rates to finance balance of payments deficits should no longer be practised; and, along with this, should be a general playing down of the usefulness of attempting to control the economy through interest rates. What is required instead is a more continuous watch by the authorities on the rate at which money and credit is created, to ensure that this purchasing power keeps in line with the real growth in GNP.

Radical Reform Required

It may be some years before the British economy is booming again, in the meantime we ought to be re-examining the means at our disposal for controlling the expansion when it comes, in order that it may not once again lead us into balance of payments deficit. One part of this re-examination should certainly be some very basic re-thinking about monetary policy. The relatively modest changes introduced so far are not radical enough. The subtleties introduced into Bank rate lending show a continued clutching at control through interest rates. When the 5% quantitative limit was withdrawn from the clearing banks, the most imaginative instrument that could be announced as taking its place was greater use of 'special deposits', which had never previously showed itself to be a particularly effective weapon, but rather more of an ancillary method of penalising banks when they did not respond to official requests.

The PIB Report tried in a very small way to set the ball rolling for future study of monetary control techniques in this country. It had itself examined the building societies and the clearing banks. But in doing so it had learnt that it was not really possible, or satisfactory, to attempt to treat institutions separately, since they were so obviously part of an inter-linked financial system. The Board therefore suggested in the final paragraph of its Bank Charges report that ' . . . these studies need to be complemented by studies of other financial institutions, with a view to clarifying the structure of the financial system and the relationships between it and the government and the monetary authorities'.

A Neddy for The City

The inquest on monetary policy may have to be carried as far as having another Royal Commission on the monetary system: but this time producing something more than just an authoritative source for quotation. A preferable alternative might be a little Neddy* for the City. Such a body would not only be able to carry out a continuing study, but would also be more likely to possess the necessary lack of reverence for established institutions and practices. The fact that an earlier effort to set up an EDC for the City miscarried should not deter a second attempt.

---

* A colloquialism for the Economic Development Committees of the National Economic Development Council.

APPENDIX
MONETARY POLICY ASPECTS OF THE EURO DOLLAR*

The continuous deficit in the US balance of payments over the past seventeen years has given to non-residents ownership of dollar balances, now in the region of $30 billion. It is from these external liabilities of the US banking system that the euro-dollar market (estimated at $13 billion) has developed since the late 1950s.

Non-resident owned balances placed in the euro-dollar market constitute a body of short term capital funds ready to move from one financial centre to another in search of the highest return. Indeed, with the inception of the euro-dollar market, short term capital movements have assumed a greater magnitude and significance. Pre-war, the flow of short term capital was composed of a multiplicity of currencies, with varying costs of forward cover and national interest rates. Today, euro-dollars provide a vast homogenous body of funds denominated in one currency (in which until quite recently there appeared little exchange risk) and having a single supply price, namely the euro-dollar rate of interest.

How Euro-dollars Are Created
Exporters of goods to America may initially accept payment for these in the form of a dollar balance in an American bank, probably in New York. But usually either personal inclination or foreign exchange regulations causes the exporter to transfer ownership of

---

* This is a re-structured version of a paper delivered by me in January 1968 to a seminar in the Sub-department of International Economics at the University of Surrey.

this dollar balance to his bank, in exchange for a credit in the domestic currency. His bank then has the alternatives of keeping the dollar balance on time deposit with a New York bank or of lending it in the euro-dollar market. If the latter is preferred, the euro-dollars may in fact be on-lent to another bank outside America. This second bank will therefore have entered on its books a liability to repay, denominated not in either banks' national currency but in US dollars. Thus a euro-dollar has been created, this being defined as a deposit liability, denominated in US dollars, of a bank outside America. The ultimate employment of the euro-dollars may be as dollars or they may be swapped into another currency, with a covering forward exchange transaction.

The euro-dollar market is exclusively inter-bank; lending is unsecured and for large round amounts (such as $1 million), but for relatively short periods of days, weeks or months. A euro-dollar may be lent many times from one bank to another before it is finally used to finance trade or investment. All the banks in a euro-dollar lending chain will record liabilities denominated in US dollars, so that on the basis of an externally owned dollar balance in New York a multiple amount of euro-dollars may be created. There is however only one balance in New York which may ultimately be employed by the final user of the euro-dollars. As the euro-dollars are on-lent, this tends to involve a matching transfer of the underlying dollar balance from one New York bank to another, depending on the American correspondent bank of the borrower. (The mechanics of euro-dollar lending and borrowing is an instruction by the lending bank to its correspondent bank in New York, where the dollar balance is held, to transfer it to the New York correspondent bank of the borrowing bank.)

Not only is *lending* in the euro-dollar market an alternative to owning a time deposit in an American bank, but *borrowing* euro-dollars is an alternative to direct borrowing from an American bank (in the days when US banks were unrestricted in their lending to non-residents). It follows from this that the euro-dollar rate of interest will lie within the limits set by American banks' time deposit and lending rates of interest. When restraint came to be placed on overseas lending by American banks, the rate charged for loans no longer effectively set an upper limit to the euro-dollar rate, since for many foreigners the alternative of borrowing in America ceased to be available.

Benefits of the Euro-dollar Market
The euro-dollar market has provided a truly international short term capital market. The high degree of mobility of euro-dollars in response to offered interest rates has added to the flow of capital from low to high interest rate countries; thus helping to even out the supply of short term capital throughout the world and bring about a greater uniformity of interest rates. Euro-dollars have also provided a supply of credit when national sources have either been inadequate or restricted.

The major use of euro-dollars is in the financing of foreign trade* and in this way has made, it is often claimed, a useful addition to international liquidity. The existence of the market has also added to international liquidity in the sense of making people more ready to hold dollar balances, since these could be employed remuneratively in the euro-dollar market. This willingness to hold dollars has lessened the desire to convert them into gold and so reduce America's reserves. It has also, incidentally, kept down the size of the US deficit, as calculated on an official settlements basis.

The euro-dollar market has, in addition, given financial institutions a greater flexibility in adjusting their cash and liquidity positions. Since London is the chief centre of the market, it has provided an added opportunity for British financial institutions to enlarge their earnings and has contributed to the development of the inter-bank market. Much of the motivation for the growth of the euro-dollar market has in fact lain in the desire of financial institutions to pursue their own self-interest, as well as seeking to satisfy their clients' needs for funds. One need not however too readily assume that, in pursuing their own interests, these financial institutions are also necessarily furthering national and international economic well-being. For although the international money market centred on the euro-dollar has added to world liquidity, it has also weakened national monetary policy and been an

* Peter Oppenheimer has estimated that euro-dollars finance about a quarter of the world's trade (The Banker, August 1967).

escalating factor in the international interest rate war.

Undesirable Side-effects
A country with a balance of payments deficit may be tempted to try and finance this by putting up its short term interest rates in order to attract foreign short term capital, much of which will be euro-dollars. To be attractive, a national interest rate must be above the rate for borrowing euro-dollars by something more than the cost of forward cover (if the host country's currency stands at a discount in the forward exchange market). Such action to attract 'hot money' has repercussions beyond any temporary benefit to the reserves. If the euro-dollars are swapped into the domestic currency they may provide an expansion of money and credit supply which is likely to be detrimental to an already unsatisfactory balance of trade position. Furthermore, the raising of its interest rates may set off competitive increases elsewhere, particularly on the part of countries losing euro-dollars. The euro-dollar rate itself is likely to be bid up, which will have implications for the American banking system and cause a rise in its lending and borrowing rates.

These side-effects of the euro-dollar market on monetary policy have already been touched upon briefly in the body of the book: it is the purpose of the remaining part of this Appendix to explore them more fully. Since, however, this is a book on "UK Monetary Policy," the case of Britain will be most frequently used for the purpose of illustration.

DEFICIT FINANCING BY HOT MONEY

Effect on Balance of Payments and Reserves

Inflows and outflows of euro-dollars, and the swapping of these into and out of sterling, have of course no effect on the UK balance of payments, since this is calculated on the basis of trade in goods and services and long term capital. Euro-dollar movements come within the short term capital position, which is only one of the methods of financing the deficit—others being international borrowing or from the reserves. When euro-dollars are accepted merely to be on-lent to foreigners, there is not even any alteration to the UK net short term capital position. However, the attraction of euro-dollar deposits into a country, and the swapping of them into the domestic currency, does have money and credit expansion effects which may ultimately contribute to deterioration in the balance of trade.

Swapping of euro-dollars into domestic currency, gives a gain to the central reserves, although this need not necessarily match the full extent of the swapping. From 1964-1967 switching of euro-dollars into sterling had been passively encouraged by the Bank of England's intervention in the foreign exchange market to keep down the cost of forward cover. Such swaps into sterling are on a short term and a covered basis; therefore, the Exchange Equalisation Account benefits only temporarily and to the same extent as the forward position deteriorates. But the Bank of England's forward position is never published and it is the favourable effect on the reserves which therefore gains the publicity. Provided UK interest rates remain attractive, forward contracts will in any case be rolled over, so that the reserves continue to benefit. The effect of this on overseas confidence depends upon just how seriously the announced monthly gold and convertible currency figures are still taken.

Countries experiencing balance of payments difficulties, thought to be temporary, have therefore often been tempted to finance their deficit (and keep it from being reflected by a fall in reserves) by raising their interest rates and attracting an inflow of short term capital, included in which has been euro-dollars. The euro-dollar rate has indeed provided a very convenient *single* international rate, against which national monetary authorities can readily gauge the required level of their own short term rates of interest if they are to attract in overseas funds. This technique of deficit financing was practised in Italy between October 1962 and September 1963. It has been used to an even greater extent by the UK since 1963 and for this reason the British example will be uppermost in mind in the remarks that follow.

Inflows of Overseas Funds: 1964–66
The use by the UK authorities of high interest rates to attract euro-dollars to finance a payments deficit can be well seen during 1964 and the early part of 1965. Bank rate was increased twice during 1964: from 4% to 5% on the 27th February and a very sharp rise from 5% to 7% on the 23rd November. During this time American interest rates hardly rose at all, the yield on the three months US Treasury bill

remaining around $3\frac{1}{2}\%$, and only moving up to $3\frac{3}{4}\%$ after the imposition by Britain of a 7% Bank rate. The euro-dollar rate similarly kept low, remaining around $4\frac{1}{4}\%$ during the greater part of 1964. It did, however, react more than the US Treasury bill did, when the UK Bank rate went up to 7%, moving up from $4\frac{1}{2}\%$ to 5%. But both these increases were comparatively mild by comparison with the steep upward rise of the UK rates.

The result of the comparatively greater rise in UK interest rates was that during 1964 and the first quarter of 1965 there was a covered arbitrage margin in Britain's favour and a considerable volume of foreign short term funds, including euro-dollars, came in during this period. At their maximum the net liabilities of UK banks in dollars were the equivalent of £400 million during the first quarter of 1965; and this equalled the extent to which our current account balance of payments was in deficit during 1964. After the first quarter of 1965, foreign funds began to be switched out of sterling again, as UK interest rates came down, while those overseas rose to a higher level.

The next period during which Britain attracted a sizeable inflow of overseas funds was in the first quarter of 1967, when the UK authorities were slower to reduce our interest rates, while the euro-dollar and American rates fell sharply, with the result that a covered arbitrage margin opened up in Britain's favour and once again the net liability of UK banks

J

in dollars increased to the equivalent of £300 million.

Extent of Swapping of Euro-dollars into Sterling
Although figures for the net liabilities in US dollars of UK banks have been quoted in the preceding paragraphs, any precise measure of the full extent to which euro-dollars are swapped into sterling is really impossible to obtain. Figures are published in the Bank of England Quarterly Bulletin which show the UK's liabilities and claims denominated in US dollars and both these categories are broken down into major countries and geographical areas. Theoretically, the extent of euro-dollars swapped into sterling should be reflected in the net liability position. The acceptance of euro-dollar deposits creates liabilities; but where these are swapped into sterling, rather than on-lent in dollars, there is no matching UK claim in dollars. However, the net liability position, while it may indicate the trend in the extent of swapping, cannot give an exact measure of it. The liability figure includes a good deal of double-counting, since a chain of on-lending of euro-dollar deposits from one UK bank to another causes them all to report dollar liabilities. Included in the claims of UK banks denominated in dollars would be their normal correspondent balances held overseas, chiefly with American banks. Also included would be any lending by the British subsidiaries of American banks (which are defined as UK banks) of euro-dollars to their American parents.

The very fact of availability of information in the

Bank of England Quarterly does however encourage some sort of hazarding of the extent of swapping, if only to refute the somewhat conservative estimates which have been given and the general tendency on the basis of these to underplay the swapping factor. In the Bank of England Quarterly Bulletin of June 1964 it was, for example, said that " . . . the amount switched into sterling is still modest in relation to the total of external liabilities; at present it is about 10%."

If one looks at recent figures available for UK banks' external liabilities and claims in US dollars, some attempt to get nearer to a more realistic estimate can be made. It is still impossible of course to ascertain the extent of double-counting in the UK liability figure. From the UK claims figure, however, UK banks' normal dollar balances overseas can be extracted, if one assumes that the bulk of these will be claims on US banks. Before Britain's move into balance of payments deficit in 1964, and the resort to a high interest rate policy to attract overseas funds, it can be seen that the level of UK claims in 1963, for example, was around £300 million. One can therefore take this figure as some measure of the amount which should be subtracted from UK claims in order to try and calculate the extent of euro-dollar swapping. The lending by British branches of American banks to their head offices may also be subtracted—but in this case from both liabilities and claims. Since this was a major feature of 1966, it may be assumed that the very large increase in UK claims from £600m. to £1,200m. which took place in that year can very largely be attributed to this factor. Pulling out these two factors gives at the end of September 1967 a UK liabilities figure denominated in US dollars of £2,600m. and a similar UK claims figure of £2,100m., providing an estimated net liabilities position of £500m., as representing the extent of swapping of euro-dollars into sterling.

Credit Expansion

The acceptance of euro-dollar deposits and the swapping of them into sterling by merchant and foreign banks in London can make possible a sudden and significant increase in the volume of credit, notably by the proceeds of such swaps being placed on deposit with hire purchase finance companies. They may also be placed on a short term basis with UK local authorities, thereby increasing either current or capital expenditure in the public sector.

Demand expansion by this means may be proceeding at a time when the authorities are attempting to restrain growth in money and credit: by open market sales of securities and directives to the clearing banks on their lending. It is no coincidence that when in the first quarter of 1965 there was the largest amount of swapping of euro-dollars into sterling, there was also such a rapid expansion of bank lending (despite an earlier appeal for restraint) that the authorities were driven in May 1965 to apply a 5% growth limit on lending by all banking institutions.

Money Supply

In many of the countries where euro-dollar deposits are accepted, the ordinary commercial banks are able, by swapping these into domestic currency, to obtain an additional cash base for the internal expansion of credit and bank deposits. UK clearing banks do not to any extent swap euro-dollar deposits into sterling so in Britain there is no immediate money supply growth effect. But, ultimately there is an increase in clearing bank deposits, as an indirect effect of the swapping of euro-dollar deposits into sterling by the non-clearing banks. In lending the proceeds of such swaps to local authorities and finance houses, the non-clearing banks are stimulating the level of economic activity, thus generating national income and therefore bank deposits. It is in this way that the clearing banks can gain deposits, despite the fact that they themselves do not swap euro-dollars into sterling.

Lender of Last Resort
Lending by accepting houses and overseas banks to the discount market can within a single quarter increase by as much as £60m. and in this way reduce the extent of the reliance of the market on the lender of last resort, thus further weakening the authorities' monetary control. The fact that the clearing banks also gain deposits through the activities of these other banking institutions increases their ability to lend to the money market.

High Interest Rates Expand Credit
The existence of euro-currency markets create other paradoxes for UK monetary policy. When the authorities raise interest rates in order to restrict credit, this also, as we have seen, has the effect of attracting euro-dollar deposits and, to the extent that these are switched into sterling, there is an increase, rather than a restriction, in the supply of credit. When UK short term rates get very high and money tight, there may even be some borrowing of euro-sterling by, for example, UK finance companies, as indicated

by Mr. Brian Oliver in his article in the Westminster Bank Review of August 1967. Sterling balances in non-resident hands are partly a result of the UK's adverse balance of payments, so that the employment of them in the euro-sterling market and lending back to the UK puts purchasing power once more in the hands of UK residents and this could cause further deterioration in the balance of trade position.

INTENSIFICATION OF INTERNATIONAL
INTEREST RATE WAR

Countries with balance of payments deficit, who seek to finance this by attracting euro-dollars, contribute to a climate of international interest rate war. The fact that euro-dollar funds exist to be attracted encourages such countries to make increases in their interest rates. As a result, other countries find themselves losing short term funds and react by putting up their interest rates; and so a tug-of-war develops, bidding up the general level of interest rates, as well as the euro-dollar rate itself. Thus, the euro-dollar market has tended to put an upward pressure on interest rates, rather than, as the Bank of England claimed ' . . . reduce interest rates in the main borrowing countries. . . . '[1]

The fact that nations calculate their balance of payments differently has the effect of stimulating this interest rate competition. If the deficit country uses the 'basic' method, as in the case of Britain, then although it cannot reduce its deficit by attracting short term capital inflow (including euro-dollars), at least it can prevent it from causing a loss of gold. But as a result of this action, another country will lose short term capital; and if it calculates its balance of payments on the 'liquidity' or 'overall' basis, as in the case of the West Germany, then this outflow will be counted as part of its payments deficit and it will seek to reduce this by raising its interest rates. Thus, although in theory one country's balance of payments deficit is another's surplus, in practice, because of the different methods of calculation, both countries can

---

[1] Bank of England Quarterly Bulletin, June 1964, page 107.

be in deficit at the same time and both will therefore adopt restrictive monetary policy, including higher interest rates.

The euro-dollar market has some very particular implications for the country whose currency it uses, causing America to react in a way which sometimes contributes to a situation of international interest rate war. To understand why this should be so, we now examine the repercussions of the existence of the euro-dollar market on the US balance of payments and the American banking system. This aspect is very fully treated in Herbert Christie's excellent article in 'The Banker'.[1]

US Balance of Payments

The euro-dollar market has in the main no effect on the American balance of payments. Euro-dollars are only part of America's already existing total external liabilities to foreigners. These external liabilities have arisen substantially from the American balance of payments deficit and not from the growth of the euro-dollar market. All that the employment of these foreign-owned balances in the euro-dollar market involves is a shift in ownership of external liabilities, not an increase in them. The shift in ownership is from foreign non-bank to foreign bank holders—and indeed often from foreign bank to foreign bank. But total external dollar liabilities remain the same; placings in the euro-dollar market do not add to short-term capital outflow and therefore do not affect the US balance of payments on a

---

[1] See 'Euro-dollars and the Balance of Payments' Herbert Christie, 'The Banker', January 1967.

liquidity basis—that is, net change in reserve assets and liquid liabilities to foreigners.

The euro-dollar market does, however, have an effect on the US balance of payments as calculated on an official settlements basis—that is, change in reserves and also in liquid and non-liquid liabilities to foreign central monetary institutions. The existence of the euro-dollar market tends to benefit the US balance of payments on an official settlements basis, since it encourages non-official holding of dollars, rather than passing them on to central banks, and thereby lessens the flow of dollars to official monetary institutions, who alone have the right to present them to the US for exchange into gold.

The only exception, where the existence of the euro-dollar market does add to the US balance of payments deficit, is when it encourages US residents to want to transfer deposits from American banks to banks abroad. Although they are discouraged from doing so, US residents are still not prohibited from placing dollars in the euro-dollar market. The official government discouragement of such practice is reinforced by American banks refusing to accept deposits from US residents for placement in the euro-dollar market. However, US private residents can place dollar balances in the euro-dollar market by going through Canadian* and Swiss banks. In the case of American corporations, who wish to place funds with their foreign subsidiaries (but still keeping within the balance of payment overseas investment guidelines),

*Any further growth of this was prevented by regulations introduced by the Canadian authorities at the beginning of May 1968.

116

American banks' overseas branches will agree to place such funds temporarily in the euro-dollar market, while awaiting allocation to the corporation's subsidiary.

US Banking System

The significance of the euro-dollar market, as far as America is concerned, lies not in the balance of payments, but in its effect on the US banking system. The euro-dollar market does not affect the money supply of America in terms of total bank deposits, but merely shifts these from one non-resident holder to another. The dollar balances employed in the euro-dollar market were already owned by foreigners and therefore the purchasing power of US residents is not further diminished by the employment of these balances in the euro-dollar market.

Such employment does, however, mean that, when placed in the euro-dollar market, foreign balances tend to shift from time to demand deposit. The reserve requirement of the American bank is therefore increased, since the amount of reserve to be held with the Federal Reserve currently varies between $12\frac{1}{2}\%$–17% for demand deposits, and 3%–6% for savings and time deposits. The effect of this on the American bank's profitability is that it no longer pays interest on the time deposit, but must keep a larger percentage of reserves against the demand deposit. A simple example will show the net effect on an individual American bank's profitability: $1 million placed in the euro-dollar market will involve a transfer from time to demand deposit, which increases the reserve requirement from $30,000 to $170,000, involving a loss of ability to earn say 7% by lending $140,000, that is $9,800. However, the US bank no longer pays 5% on the $1 million time deposit, that is $50,000, so there is a net improvement in profitability of $40,200.

But for the American banking system as a whole, the effect of the employment of dollar balances in the euro-dollar market is unfavourable. By increasing the average reserve requirement (due to the shift from time to demand deposit) it reduces the extent to which bank deposits can be created on a given cash base: for example, a 3% reserve requirement enables the US banking system as a whole to create deposits $33\frac{1}{3}$ times the cash held in the banking system, whereas a 17% reserve requirement reduces this multiple to 6 times.

To resist this transfer from time to demand deposit, which increases their reserve requirement, American banks will try to keep their deposit rates attractive in relation to the euro-dollar rate. In recent years, since their loan rates have not risen as much, this has tended to narrow the spread between deposit and lending rates and this again has had a detrimental effect on banks' profitability.

When the rates offered by American banks on time deposit reach the Regulation Q maximum, any further competition for deposits must then be transferred to the euro-dollar market. In doing so, American banks can only gain deposits from one another, via the euro-dollar market, by having their overseas branches bid for euro-dollars and then lend these back to the head office.

It can therefore be seen that US time deposit rates have to match to some extent the upward movement in the euro-dollar rate (as far as Regulation Q permits), if the American banking system is not to experience a loss of time deposits and an increase in reserve requirement. When, during periods of credit scarcity, their competition for deposits shifts from the domestic to the external sphere, the American banks themselves bid for euro-dollars and contribute to the rise in the rate, which in turn further lessens the attractiveness of their own time deposit rates. Thus there are elements of interaction and indeed escalation.

It is therefore the impact of the euro-dollar market on the American banking system which aggravates the international interest rate war, and not any unfavourable effect on the US balance of payments—for in the main there is none.

INDEX

Date Due